Andrew Johnson

17th President of the United States

A stern, fiercely patriotic man, Andrew Johnson inherited the presidency after the tragic death of Abraham Lincoln. Johnson's four years in the White House were marked by betrayal and disappointment. (Library of Congress.)

Andrew Johnson

17th President of the United States

Rita Stevens

 GARRETT EDUCATIONAL CORPORATION

Manufactured in the United States of America

Edited and produced by Synthegraphics Corporation

Library of Congress Cataloging in Publication Data

Stevens, Rita.
  Andrew Johnson, 17th president of the United States.

  (Presidents of the United States)
  Bibliography: p.
  Includes index.
  Summary: Traces the life and career of the statesman who became president following the assassination of Abraham Lincoln.
    1. Johnson, Andrew, 1808–1875—Juvenile literature.   2. Presidents—United States—Biography—Juvenile literature.   [1. Johnson, Andrew, 1808–1875.   2. Presidents] I. Title.   II. Title: Andrew Johnson, seventeenth president of the United States.   III. Series.
  E667.S73   1989   973.8'1'0924   [B]   [92]   88-28487
  ISBN 0-944483-16-X

Contents

Chronology for Andrew Johnson

1808 Born on December 29

1822 Became a tailor's apprentice

1826 Moved with family to Greeneville, Tennessee; opened a tailor shop

1827 Married Eliza McCardle on May 17

1828–1833 Served as alderman and then mayor of Greeneville

1835–1841 Served two terms as a member of Tennessee House of Representatives

1841–1843 Member of Tennessee State Senate

1843–1853 Served five terms in U.S. House of Representatives

1853–1857 Elected twice to governorship of Tennessee

1857–1862 Elected by Tennessee state legislature to serve in U.S. Senate

1862–1864 Served as military governor of Tennessee

1864 Elected Vice-President of the United States

1865 Became 17th President of the United States on April 15, after Lincoln's assassination

1868 Stood impeachment trial in U.S. Senate; was acquitted of all charges

1869, 1872 Tried and failed to win seats in U.S. Senate and House of Representatives

1874 Elected to U.S. Senate

1875 Died on July 31 in Tennessee

Chapter 1

The President Is Dead!

April 14, 1865, dawned as a day of hope and promise in Washington, D.C. For four long years, the northern states, called the Union, had been locked in a bloody civil war with the southern states, called the Confederacy. Now the end of that terrible conflict was in sight.

Just five days earlier, Confederate General Robert E. Lee had surrendered to Union General Ulysses S. Grant at Appomattox, Virginia. The night after Lee's surrender, jubilant crowds gathered on the White House lawn to hear President Abraham Lincoln speak of his hopes for the harmonious reunion of North and South. And, in the days that followed, a mood of optimism and rejoicing filled the nation's capital and the entire North.

One who shared this mood was Andrew Johnson of Tennessee, Lincoln's Vice-President. During the war years, Johnson had been despised as a traitor in his native South because of his unswerving loyalty to the Union. Lincoln had rewarded that loyalty by choosing Johnson for the office of Vice-President. Now Johnson hoped to put the bitterness of war behind him and join in the work of knitting together a renewed, stronger union of all the states.

However, not all of Washington's inhabitants shared this

hopeful mood. Those who had sympathized with the Confederacy were filled with despair at its defeat and fear for the future of the South. One of these southern sympathizers was a handsome, well-known actor named John Wilkes Booth. During the final months of the war, Booth had secretly tried to form a conspiracy to kidnap Lincoln and hold him prisoner in the South for the ransom of Confederate soldiers who had been imprisoned in the North. But this plan came to nothing.

The night following Lee's surrender, Booth stood in the crowd that had gathered on the White House lawn to hear Lincoln talk about bringing the South back into the Union. Seething with rage, Booth turned to his friend Lewis Payne and said quietly, "That is the last speech Lincoln will ever make." He called Payne and a handful of other conspirators back to his hotel room and unveiled the details of a new, desperate, and deadly plan.

A TRAGIC GOOD FRIDAY

April 14 was Good Friday. Holiday or not, Vice-President Johnson had a busy day planned. In his room at a hotel called the Kirkwood House, he awoke early, as he usually did. After a simple breakfast, he and his secretary, William Browning, went to the Capitol building, where Johnson found his desk covered with papers that needed his attention.

Later that morning, Johnson attended a meeting of Lincoln's Cabinet, the men who advise the President on official matters. Johnson talked briefly with Lincoln after the meeting, before the President left to take Mrs. Lincoln for a carriage drive around the city. It was the last time Johnson and Lincoln spoke to each other.

Johnson remained busy all day. He and Browning snatched a hasty lunch and then continued working in Johnson's office. Upon their return to Kirkwood House at about five o'clock, Browning was told that a visitor had called for him during the afternoon and left his card. Browning looked at the card curiously. It was from John Wilkes Booth, the actor, whom Browning had once met in Nashville, Tennessee, but knew only slightly. Scribbled on the card was the message, "Don't wish to disturb you — are you at home?" Shrugging, Browning put the card in his pocket as Johnson went into the dining room for dinner.

A Nervous Assassin

In the meantime, George Atzerodt, another guest at Kirkwood House, had spent an anxious day. He was a middle-aged, undistinguished coach-maker who had registered at the hotel that very morning — getting a room close to Johnson's.

Atzerodt was one of Booth's fellow conspirators. Booth had decided upon a wild plan: to assassinate the President, the Vice-President, the Cabinet members, and Union General Ulysses S. Grant. Atzerodt was assigned to track and kill Andrew Johnson.

Apparently, however, Atzerodt lacked the feverish fanaticism of Booth. He was nervous and frightened at the thought of the violent and dangerous act of assassination. He thought, however, that perhaps he could work up enough courage to do the deed.

After leaving his pistol and some papers in his hotel room, Atzerodt hurried to the bar in Kirkwood House for a drink to stiffen his nerve. Then he moved on to a tavern for another drink, and then to another tavern for still another drink, and then more of the same. His hand trembled each time he raised his glass. Before long, he knew, he must return to Kirkwood House to carry out his part of the assassination plan.

Ford's Theatre

After finishing his dinner, Johnson prepared to go to bed early. He was tired and felt rather unwell; he had been fighting an attack of fever ever since his inauguration as Vice-President a month earlier. But Leonard Farwell, a friend and former governor of Wisconsin, dropped by to visit. Before long, though, Farwell told Johnson that he must be off. He was going to Ford's Theatre to see the famous actress Laura Keane in the play *Our American Cousin*.

It was well known that the President and Mrs. Lincoln would also be attending Ford's Theatre that evening. Farwell hoped to have a moment's conversation with Lincoln between acts of the play. After his departure, Johnson promptly went to bed.

The play at Ford's Theatre was in its third act when Farwell heard a shot ring out, followed by a woman's scream. An instant later, John Wilkes Booth leaped from the President's special box onto the stage, brandishing a pistol. Like the rest of the audience, Farwell sat for a moment stunned and confused, wondering whether this was part of the play. Then Booth ran off the stage as a woman cried, "The President has been shot!"

Farwell kept his head. He shoved through the milling, shrieking crowd in the theater. Fearing for the life of his friend, Andrew Johnson, Farwell rushed two blocks to Kirkwod House. He then ran up the stairs and pounded furiously on Johnson's door. There was no answer. Was he too late?

THE LONG NIGHT

The Vice-President was roused from his sleep by a thunderous hammering on the door. "Johnson!" someone was shouting. "If you are in there, I must see you at once!" As Johnson

Actor John Wilkes Booth shot President Abraham Lincoln at Ford's Theatre in Washington on the night of April 14, 1865, just a few days after the end of the Civil War. (Library of Congress.)

opened the door, he was surprised to see Farwell leaping into the air, trying to look through the small transom window above the door. "Thank God you are alive!" cried Farwell when he saw his friend. After Johnson let him into the room, Farwell told him that someone had shot Lincoln.

Although for a moment he thought Farwell was playing a joke on him, Johnson quickly realized the seriousness of the situation. The two men paced nervously around the room, unsure of what to do. Johnson wanted to go find out what was happening, but Farwell persuaded him to stay, pointing out that his life might be in danger, too.

A Conspiracy Unveiled

Soon Farwell and Johnson heard the sound of voices and hurrying footsteps. Then someone knocked on the door, but Farwell refused to open it until he recognized the voice of a congressman. The congressman told Johnson that a worried crowd had come to the hotel to make sure the Vice-President was all right. He then agreed to wait with Johnson while Farwell went back to Ford's Theatre to get the latest news about Lincoln's condition.

However, Farwell returned in only a few moments. He was accompanied by Major James O'Beirne, the commander of the military detachment that had been assigned to keep order in the capital during the war. O'Beirne advised Johnson to remain safely in his hotel room with friends. After all, he pointed out, assassins might still be lying in wait to attack the Vice-President. But Johnson insisted that he must go to the President. He threw on a hat and coat and, with Farwell leading and O'Beirne following, set off in the dark to walk to the theater.

Meanwhile, Secretary of War Edwin Stanton had taken action. As soon as he was notified of the shooting, he sent a note to Salmon P. Chase, the Chief Justice of the Supreme Court, telling him to be ready to swear in Johnson as President. He also sent a guard to Kirkwood House to protect Johnson.

The guard, John Lee, learned from someone at the hotel that a guest named Atzerodt had been asking questions about the Vice-President. Lee went to Atzerodt's room and knocked, but received no answer. He then broke down the door. Inside the room he found a pistol and some cartridges, one of Booth's bankbooks, a large knife, and a map of Virginia. Lee knew at once that the mysterious Mr. Atzerodt was connected with Booth and that the assassination plot had been aimed at Johnson as well as at Lincoln.

However, because he had spent the whole day and much of the night in bars, Atzerodt was too drunk and too frightened to carry out his share of the plot. It is now believed that Booth's mysterious visit to the hotel during the previous afternoon was an attempt to find out Browning's and Johnson's plans for the evening, so that Booth could assign another, more reliable, conspirator to do away with the Vice-President.

Lewis Payne proved bolder than the miserable Atzerodt. He attacked Secretary of State William Seward, savagely wounding him in the neck with a knife. Only the fact that Seward was still wearing a bandage from an earlier neck injury saved his life; the bandage turned Payne's blow away. Seward was not killed, although he was badly hurt. Several other members of his household were hurt when they attempted to seize Payne, but the would-be assassin fled into the night.

The Deathwatch

Johnson was brought to the house across from Ford's Theatre where the gravely wounded President was lying. Lincoln had been shot in the head, and doctors did not expect him to recover consciousness. The Vice-President stepped into the bedroom where Lincoln lay dying and looked for the final time upon the face of his friend and leader. He had once called Lincoln "the greatest American." Now he knew that in a few short hours he would have to shoulder Lincoln's burden of leadership. But Lincoln, pale and unconscious, could offer no guidance now—not even a farewell.

Robert Lincoln, the President's older son, was there.

Johnson took Robert's hand and spoke quietly to him for a moment. Then, as Johnson left the house, he came upon Mary Lincoln, the President's wife, in an outer room. Mrs. Lincoln's shock and grief were immense; she had suffered from hysterics so severe that she had to be removed from the bedroom where her husband lay. In silence, Johnson held her hand briefly. He then went back through the dark streets and the weeping crowds to Kirkwood House to wait for the grim news that he knew would come at any moment.

Five hours later, at about 7:30 on the morning of April 15, 1865, Lincoln died. Immediately, someone ran to Kirkwood House and gasped out the tragic message: "The President is dead!" A few minutes later, Johnson received an official notice that had been prepared hours earlier by Secretary of the Treasury Hugh McCulloch. The last paragraph of the notice read:

> By the death of President Lincoln the office of President has devolved under the Constitution upon you. The emergency of the government demands that you should immediately qualify according to the requirements of the Constitution, and enter upon the duties of President of the United States. If you will please make known your pleasure such arrangements as you deem proper will be made.

THE NEW PRESIDENT

Johnson agreed with the Cabinet that he should take the oath of office as soon as possible, in order to keep the government running smoothly. Matters were arranged quickly. A public inauguration, it was felt, would be in poor taste on such a sorrowful occasion. So, just three hours after Lincoln's death, Johnson was sworn in before a dozen witnesses in his hotel room.

Because of the tragedy of Lincoln's death, Johnson did not have the festive public inauguration that had become customary. This engraving from an 1865 newspaper shows Johnson (in the center, facing outward) receiving the oath of office from Chief Justice Salmon P. Chase in a room of the Kirkwood House. (Library of Congress.)

Chief Justice Chase delivered the oath of office to the man whom, only a few weeks before, he had sworn in as Vice-President. Johnson was "apparently calm, but very grave," Chase later recalled. He swore to preserve, protect, and defend the Constitution, and then he kissed the Bible that Chase held up. Chase said, "You are President. May God support, guide, and bless you in your arduous duties." Andrew Johnson, whose background was more humble than that of any President before or since, had become the first Vice-President to attain the presidency as the result of an assassination.

Johnson spoke in a subdued voice to the witnesses, telling them that Lincoln's assassination had nearly overwhelmed him. He asked for their help and support, promising to work hard and do his best as President. He repeated that request and that promise later in the day, at his first Cabinet meeting. He knew that great difficulties lay ahead of him as he faced the task of rebuilding a nation and a people shattered by war.

It is probably fortunate that, on that first day of his presidency, Andrew Johnson could not foresee just how difficult his task was going to be. He would face accusations, treacheries, and conflicts on all sides. Strife and political infighting would bedevil his administration, strip him of all real power, and make him perhaps the most misunderstood leader the United States has ever had. And he would be the only President ever to be impeached and stand trial for crimes committed in office.

Chapter 2

Runaway

No President of the United States reached that high office from a more humble background than Andrew Johnson. Even Abraham Lincoln, the rail-splitter from the prairie, had a more fortunate start in life than Johnson. Lincoln's family was poor, but at least they always had a home of their own, and Lincoln was able to go to school for a few months. Johnson's family, on the other hand, lived in a borrowed shack, and he never had a day of formal schooling.

By sheer determination and hard work, however, Johnson made himself into a prosperous, well-read man and a successful politician. But in many ways, the key to his character—and to his political downfall—lies in the enormous difficulties he faced during his early years.

A MUDSILL FAMILY

Not much is known about Andrew Johnson's family background. His father, Jacob Johnson, was a man of mixed English, Scottish, and Irish ancestry who arrived in Raleigh, the small but fast-growing town that was the state capital of North Carolina, in about 1800. Some people later said that Jacob Johnson had been born in northern England and had grown up and worked there before making his way to Boston and then moving south. Others said he was from Virginia.

Whatever his origins, Johnson soon made a place for himself in Raleigh. He was a tall, easy-going, good-natured man who could not read or write but could turn his hand to many sorts of work. After arriving in Raleigh, he found a job as a waiter and handyman at an inn owned by Peter Casso.

Over the next 10 years, Johnson held a variety of part-time and odd jobs. He was a bank janitor; a town constable; the ringer of the town bell that announced weddings, fires, and funerals; and sexton, or caretaker, of the Presbyterian church. He was even the captain of the local volunteer militia troop for a while. But none of these jobs paid very well – or perhaps Jacob Johnson was just not very good at managing money. His family was among the town's poorest.

In 1801, about a year after he came to Raleigh, Jacob Johnson married a Scottish-Irish girl named Mary McDonough. Little is known of her except that she was small, slender, and dark-haired. Like her husband, she signed their marriage license with an "X" because she could not write.

Mary Johnson, or "Polly," as she was called, helped her husband with his work at Casso's Inn, waiting on tables and lending a hand in the kitchen when extra help was needed. She also worked as a laundress, washing, ironing, and mending shirts and clothing for many of the town's more well-to-do citizens, including some of the state senators from the capitol building across the road.

Because the Johnsons were good workers, Mr. Casso let them live in a little shack or cottage in the courtyard of the inn. There they set up housekeeping. The house, like the houses of most laborers and poor people at that time and place, had a floor of packed earth. Poor families were sometimes called "mudsill" families, after their earthen sills, or doorways.

A Good Deed Brings Bad Luck

The Johnson's first child, a son, was born in 1804. They named him William. A second child, a daughter, died as a baby; her name, if she had one, was not recorded, Their third and last child was born on December 29, 1808. Casso's Inn was busy with merrymakers during the holiday season, and Jacob Johnson worked late that night, until he received word that his second son had been born. He and Mary named the boy Andrew, perhaps after a relative of his mother. The child usually was called Andy.

Now that he had two small children to support, Jacob Johnson worked at whatever jobs he could find when he was not busy at Casso's. He also enjoyed socializing with the men of Raleigh, however, and his friendly ways made him popular even with some of the town's wealthier citizens. In December of 1811, when Andy was three, his father accompanied Colonel Thomas Henderson, editor of a local newspaper, and some other men on a fishing outing to a place called Hunter's Mill, several miles from Raleigh. The events of that day made Jacob Johnson a hero—and cost him his life.

Henderson and two other men were in a small boat. One of the high-spirited fishermen began rocking the boat, but the fun ended when the boat overturned. One of Henderson's friends, unable to swim, panicked and clutched the newspaper editor in a dangerous grip. Both men went under and were near drowning.

On the bank of the stream, Johnson saw the two men vanish beneath the surface of the icy water. He plunged in, swam underwater until he located them, and managed to pull them both to shore. But by the time he and his grateful friends returned to Raleigh, Johnson was badly chilled. He caught a cold, which developed into a long illness that he could not shake off. A year later, while ringing the town bell to an-

In 1865, the magazine Harper's Weekly *published this drawing of the humble home in Raleigh, North Carolina, in which Andrew Johnson was born.* (Library of Congress.)

nounce a funeral, he collapsed. He died soon after, on January 4, 1813.

A week later, Henderson's paper, the *Raleigh Star,* published a death notice that praised Jacob Johnson's "honesty, industry, and humane and friendly disposition." Henderson also wrote, "No one laments his death more than the editor of this paper, for he owes his life to the boldness and humanity of Johnson." Kind though they were, these words were little help to Mary Johnson, now a widow with boys of eight and four to feed.

Tailor's Apprentice

Some of the townspeople of Raleigh helped the Johnsons with food and other gifts, but Mary Johnson knew that she would have to find a way to take care of her young family herself. She acquired a hand loom and began weaving and selling cloth in addition to her other work. Two years later, she found a place for Bill, Andy's older brother, as an apprentice.

The system of apprenticeship that was used in the United States at that time was modeled on a system that had been used for several centuries in Europe. A tradesman who needed help would take a youngster as an apprentice. The apprentice was bound over to, or legally committed to the care of, the tradesman for a given number of years – usually until the apprentice was 21. During those years, the apprentice worked for the tradesman, and any income he earned or property he acquired belonged to his master. For his part, the tradesman provided food and lodging for the apprentice and taught him the skills of his trade.

The apprenticeship system had both good and bad features. Poor families who apprenticed a son were relieved of the need to feed and clothe him. And boys who became apprentices often stood a good chance of becoming skilled tradesmen themselves one day. But the system was sometimes abused by masters who wanted only to get as much work out of their apprentices as possible. And some masters were extremely cruel to their apprentices. Even with a kind master, however, apprenticeship must often have seemed a bit like slavery to the hard-working teenage apprentices, or boundboys, as they were sometimes called.

At first, Bill was apprenticed to Jacob Johnson's friend Colonel Henderson. But Henderson died, and Bill's apprenticeship in the printing shop of the newspaper ended. Mary Johnson then apprenticed Bill to the local tailor, James J. Selby. Around this time, Mary remarried. Unfortunately, because her new husband, a man named Turner Dougherty, either could not find a job or was not a good worker, Mary soon found herself working to support him.

Mary had little time to spend with Andy, who roamed the streets and the countryside on his own from an early age. Schools cost money, and there was no money to spare for an education for Andy. Because he was inquisitive and curious, Andy probably would have been an excellent student. He was a dark-haired, dark-eyed boy, rather short but well-built and strong, with a friendly but stubborn personality. Andy resented his "mudsill" family's low status in the community, but there was not much that he could do about it.

In February of 1822, just after Andy turned 13, tailor Selby offered to take him as an apprentice, too. Mary Johnson agreed and made her mark on the necessary legal paper, called the articles of apprenticeship. Andy then went to join his brother and the other workers at Selby's tailor shop.

Young Andy had no particular interest in tailoring and no desire to work while other boys he knew were hunting and fishing in the nearby woods and streams. But his new position did have one outstanding attraction. Workmen in shops of the time often hired a reader—or took turns among themselves, if they could read—to entertain them as they worked. The reader would read aloud from newspapers, novels, plays, books of speeches and sermons, and anything else that came to hand. Even before he was apprenticed to Selby, Andy used to come around to the shop from time to time just to sit with Bill and listen to the readers. Now he could listen to them all day long, every day.

A Piecemeal Education

Andy Johnson's education, such as it was, began during his apprenticeship at Selby's. He listened with pleasure to everything that was read, but his favorites were newspapers and political essays. These opened a window onto the wide world beyond Raleigh and introduced Andy to the men and ideas that shaped history. His delight in listening soon grew into a desire to read for himself. Although he could not attend school, he did find teachers who were able to point him in the right direction.

James Litchford, the shop foreman, gave Andy a primer (a book for beginning readers) and taught him the alphabet. Dr. William Hill, one of the town's most prominent and educated citizens, thought it admirable that a poor and ignorant boy wanted to improve himself. So Dr. Hill would come to the shop now and then to read to Andy and encourage him.

One of the hired readers, possibly touched by the boy's passionate interest in books, gave Andy an old, worn copy of *The American Speaker.* This was a collection of famous political speeches. Dr. Hill then gave Andy a book of speeches by the great English statesmen William Pitt and Charles James Fox. Andy learned some of the speeches in these books by heart and, in spare moments snatched from his work, he repeated them over and over to himself while studying the printed words. Eventually, by memory and sheer, stubborn persistence, Andy taught himself to read. His vocabulary was poor, and he still could not write, but he generally managed to puzzle the meaning out of any book he could find.

ON THE ROAD

As a small child, Andy Johnson led a very independent life. His mother was busy working day and night, and his brother, Bill, was sent away as an apprentice when Andy was five or six years old. So he grew used to coming and going as he pleased and doing what he wanted.

Some of the townspeople called Andy wild and undisciplined. Later, these people recalled that young Johnson ran around with a rowdy group of youths. But this much is certain: Andy was stubborn, proud, and independent—and these qualities were not likely to make him happy as an apprentice.

His tasks at the tailor shop were simple at first. He was taught to cut cloth and to smooth the pieces with a heavy iron. Later, he was taught the different stitches (all done by hand, of course, as the sewing machine had not yet been invented) and how to sew the pieces together into garments. To tailor Selby's surprise, Andy developed a real skill and became one of the best workers in the shop.

As masters went, Selby was not a bad one. He did not work his apprentices any harder than was the custom, and he gave them occasional holidays from work. But after two years, Andy grew increasingly rebellious and impatient to be out on his own. Perhaps his naturally independent spirit was fired by his political readings. However, he was only 15 years old, and his apprenticeship had more than five years still to run. What was he to do?

Flight in the Night

In June of 1824, Andy took action. He ran away, breaking his apprenticeship and becoming a fugitive from the law. There are two stories about why he ran away. According to one, Selby insulted Andy, who struck his master, then fled for fear of revenge. Another says that Andy and some other youths were throwing stones at the house of an old woman who had called them "mudsills" and "trash" the day before. One of the stones broke a window, and the boys fled for fear of arrest.

Whatever his reasons, Andy left town one night that June. Bill went with him, and two other apprentices may have accompanied them for a short while. They returned to Selby's just long enough to put on their newest clothes and gather up their tailoring tools (which belonged to Selby) and Andy's few dog-eared books. Then they set off along the nearest road.

At first, everyone expected the two fugitives to return, shamefaced and apologetic, within a day or two. But when they did not come back, Selby ran an advertisement in the *Raleigh Gazette*, offering a reward for them. It said: "Ran away from the Subscriber, on the night of the 15th instant, two apprentice boys, legally bound, named William and Andrew Johnson." Selby offered a reward of $10 for the return of both boys, and added, "I will give the above Reward for Andrew Johnson alone."

Some historians have suggested from this advertisement that Andrew must have been a good tailor, and therefore very valuable to Selby, as the master was willing to give the whole reward for him. It is more likely, however, that Selby was willing to pay for Andrew alone because William's apprenticeship had almost expired anyway.

Carthage and Laurens

In two or three days, the Johnson boys had walked as far as Carthage, North Carolina, a town about 75 miles from Raleigh. There Andy found a vacant shack and hung out a sign, advertising himself as a tailor. He managed to make enough money to support himself and his brother, but he was uneasy. He felt Carthage was too close to Raleigh for comfort.

Perhaps Selby would hear of Andy's new business and come to force him back to Raleigh to finish his apprenticeship – the law was on Selby's side. So, after a brief stay in Carthage, the boys packed up their belongings and crossed the state line into South Carolina. They settled in a town called Laurens.

Once again, Andy set up shop as a tailor. Although Bill was older, he was content to leave all of the decisions – and most of the work — to his younger brother. Bill Johnson didn't look much like Andy. He was tall, freckle-faced, and light-haired. And he lacked the younger boy's burning ambition and pride. In many ways, Bill resembled his father, Jacob Johnson. Like Jacob, he was easy-going and friendly, and he seemed willing to accept his lowly position in life.

Andrew, however, resented the fact that other people looked down on him because of his lack of wealth and social standing. Such people included many who did not have to work as hard for their livings as he did. He had an especially painful experience of this sort in Laurens. Andy fell in love with a pretty girl named Sarah Word, one of the most popular girls in town. It seems that she returned his feelings, for the two spent much time together. Andy helped her design and sew a quilt, and he carved his initials into a chair on her porch.

However, when Andy asked for permission to marry Sarah, her mother broke up the relationship. She made it clear that she had no intention of allowing her daughter to marry a vagabond with no money and a mysterious background. Sarah dutifully rejected Andrew.

Because his feelings were deeply injured and his pride was hurt, Andy decided to leave Laurens. As always, Bill agreed to Andrew's plans, and the two set off on the road once again.

Return to Raleigh

During the bleak months that followed, Andrew roamed restlessly here and there, unwilling to settle down and risk another humiliation. Before long, Bill grew tired of such a footloose life. Because his apprenticeship had expired, he was safe from Selby and the law. So Bill decided to return to Raleigh on his own. But Andrew could not yet bring himself to go home and face possible punishment.

Instead, Andrew followed where the road led — into the western part of the Carolinas and perhaps beyond. In later years, many people said that he had passed through Mississippi and Alabama. In fact, after he became famous, towns across the South claimed that Andrew Johnson had worked in them when he was young and on the road.

But because he never spoke about these months of wandering, it is not known exactly where Andy went or how he spent his time. It is likely, though, that he was impressed by the rough-and-ready life of the frontier region, where social distinctions were less important than in the older, more settled towns. Moreover, this was where a man could build a new life for himself through hard work and ambition.

But Andrew could not put out of his mind the knowledge that he had unfinished business to take care of back in Raleigh. He would be forever branded as a coward and a runaway unless he returned to his hometown and to Selby. Furthermore, he knew that his mother needed his help. Both Bill and his stepfather, Turner Dougherty, were too irresponsible or lazy to take care of her. So, in 1826, at the age of 17, Andrew went back to Raleigh, after an absence of two years.

A Cool Welcome

The returning runaway may have been burning with the desire to set things right and clear his name, but he did not receive a warm welcome from his master, Selby. The tailor had moved to a new shop about 20 miles from town, so Andrew hiked out to talk to him. To his dismay, he was told that Selby had no need for his services any longer, so the tailor would not take him back.

Selby then warned Andrew that if the young man went to work for himself or for anyone else, anything he earned would belong to Selby by law. The only solution was for Andrew to buy out the remaining years of his apprenticeship with a cash payment to Selby. But this was impossible, for Andrew had no money.

Here was an unbearable situation: Andrew could not work for his master, nor could he buy his way out of his apprenticeship. And he could not earn money to set himself free because his earnings would belong legally to his master!

To make matters worse, Andy found his family in a terrible state. His mother was greatly aged and worn, partly by debts and hard work and partly, as Andrew knew, by worry about her runaway sons. Bill and Dougherty contributed little or nothing to the household, so Andrew accepted responsibility as head of the family.

Andy could have made a living as a tailor. James Litchford, Selby's former foreman who had taught Andy the alphabet, had opened his own shop and offered the boy a job. But Andrew was afraid that if he had a steady job, Selby would take legal measures to seize his earnings. So he skulked around town, looking for odd jobs at Casso's Inn and elsewhere, as his father had done before him.

On some days Andy earned a few coins; on others, he was lucky to take scraps of food from the inn home for his mother. The whole family was mired in the worst poverty they had ever known. Many years later, Andrew Johnson spoke about these dismal days. He called poverty a "gaunt and haggard monster" and said that he met this monster everywhere he turned, "in the day and in the night."

A NEW START

In this desperate and unhappy situation, Andrew's thoughts turned to the frontier communities west of the Carolinas. He knew that out there he could earn a living and the family could start a new life. He had come back to Raleigh hoping to clear himself with Selby. He was even willing to work out the rest of his apprenticeship. But because Selby would not take him back, Andy now decided that there was nothing to prevent him from moving away.

Some of Mary Johnson Dougherty's relatives had gone west to Tennessee, and word had reached the family that this was a good place to settle. So Andrew obtained a weary old horse and a broken-down two-wheeled cart. One August day in 1826, with their few possessions piled atop the cart, the two boys, their mother, and their stepfather trudged out of Raleigh on the dusty road that led westward along the Daniel Boone Trail to Tennessee. The trip ahead wouldn't be easy, but Andrew Johnson knew one thing: he would be his own boss from now on.

Chapter 3

A Politician for the Common People

On the day they left Raleigh, Johnson's family covered almost 30 miles. Because the cart could not carry them all, they took turns riding on top of the pile of household goods, walking with the horse between turns. That night, they stayed at the farm of a family named Craig, near Chapel Hill.

From then on, as the road became increasingly rugged, they were forced to travel more slowly. In some places they had to haul the cart out of deep mud after thunderstorms, or cross raging streams. Occasionally they traveled for a few days with another family or two, but most of the time they were on their own, camping by the roadside. The hills became mountains, difficult and tiring to climb. At night, wildcats and bears prowled the woods; Johnson shot one bear that was about to charge the campfire.

The trip was hard on all four travelers, but especially on Andy's mother. He knew that she was near the limit of her strength. Then one afternoon in September they arrived at Greeneville, a town in a pleasant valley in East Tennessee. Andy announced that they would go no farther; Greeneville was to be their new home.

A day or two later, Johnson left the family campsite and

went into town to rent a cabin. He saw a group of girls on their way home from school, the Rhea Academy, and asked one of them if she knew where he might find a place to rent. The girl—who was brown-haired, tall, and pretty—was gracious to Johnson, in spite of his vagabond appearance. She even introduced him to a man who had some cabins to rent. This man, it turned out, owned a general store and had some fabric in stock. Learning that Jonson was a tailor, the man offered to pay Andy to make clothes out of this material. In one day, Johnson had found a place to live, his first job in Greeneville—and his future wife.

The schoolgirl who was so kind to Johnson was named Eliza McCardle. Her father had been the town shoemaker, but he was dead, and Eliza lived with her widowed mother. Johnson soon began courting her and was overjoyed to find that she liked him as much as he liked her. This time, it appeared that no obstacles would stand in the couple's way. Johnson had been able to find work, and he quickly made friends and won a place for himself in the community.

A few months later, Greeneville's town tailor retired. Johnson thereupon rented a two-room building on the main street and put up a sign that announced: "A. Johnson, Tailor."

Not long afterward, on May 17, 1827, Johnson and Eliza were married. He was 18; she was 16. The ceremony took place in the home of Eliza's mother. It was performed by the local justice of the peace, Mordecai Lincoln, who was a distant relative of Abraham Lincoln and who became one of Johnson's best friends.

The newlyweds moved into Johnson's rented home and tailor shop. He then bought a small farm outside town for his mother and stepfather. Bill, his brother, was something of a ne'er-do-well. After working for a time as a carpenter in Greeneville, he drifted west and eventually ended up in Texas, where he remained.

Johnson opened his own tailor shop in Greeneville, Tennessee, not long after his arrival there. His skill and hard work soon brought him a good living and allowed him to support a family. (Library of Congress.)

TOWN POLITICS

At first, Johnson was kept busy establishing himself in business and earning enough money to support himself and his wife. Eliza proved to be a thrifty, shrewd businesswoman who took charge of the family finances and helped Johnson prosper.

Eliza was an asset to her husband in another way, too. She greatly admired his ambition and his determination to rise above his humble origins, and she was able to help him by completing his education. In the evening, after his day's work was done, Johnson sat with his wife in their tiny room behind the shop and traced out letters and numbers by lamp-light. Within a few years, he had learned to write and had mastered basic arithmetic. He was not much of a speller — but, in those days, few people bothered about spelling.

Jacksonian Democracy

Before long, Johnson's hard work and honesty had made him one of the town's most respected tradesmen. He always completed work on time and would not accept payment for a garment until he was sure that it fit properly. (For his own part, he dressed neatly but plainly in black suits that he stitched himself.) As the months passed, Johnson became increasingly certain that Greeneville was a good place for him. And as he felt more and more secure, he began expressing his political beliefs in discussions and debates with the townspeople.

At the time, the social structure of East Tennessee was much different from that of Johnson's hometown of Raleigh. Although there were some wealthy, aristocratic, slave-owning families in Greeneville, they were not as numerous as in North Carolina. Much of East Tennessee consisted of small farms, owned by families who worked the soil themselves, or with only one or two slaves. Laboring men and tradesmen were proud of themselves and did not believe that they ought to feel inferior to the upper class.

A movement called Jacksonian democracy — after Andrew Jackson, a Tennesseean who would be elected President in 1828 — was taking shape throughout the land. Jacksonian democracy encouraged the common people, such as the laborers, farmers, and backwoodsmen of East Tennessee, to insist on their rights and to participate in political life.

In general, Jacksonian democracy was promoted by the Democratic Party. The Whig Party, on the other hand, tended

Johnson married Eliza McCardle in 1827. She was ill in later life and did not often appear in public during her husband's presidency, when this engraving was made. (Library of Congress.)

to support old, established values and politicians from wealthy or aristocratic backgrounds. In 1828, for the first time, it seemed to Democrats like Johnson that it was possible for political power to pass from the aristocrats, merchants, and landowners into the hands of the working class. It was the perfect time for Andrew Johnson to enter politics.

Johnson was excited by the winds of change blowing

across the nation. Andrew Jackson — a poor boy originally from South Carolina who had achieved prosperity and political importance — was Johnson's hero. To the growing circle of friends who gathered for conversations and debates in his shop, the young tailor proclaimed himself proud to be a member of the common, working class. People who earned their livings "by the sweat of their brow," as he liked to put it, were more worth knowing than those who were lazy and idle and never had to work.

Alderman Johnson

Johson's best friend was Blackston McDannel, a genial plasterer with a lively sense of humor. Their friendship was a lifelong one. McDannel remained a simple plasterer after Johnson had become a figure of national importance. Nevertheless, the two continued to exchange letters full of jokes and honest, open comradeship.

Another new friend was Sam Milligan, a student at a local college. Johnson met Milligan at a meeting of the college's debating club. Although it meant a round trip of eight miles, sometimes in bad weather, Johnson attended most of the club's weekly debates. He began to show real talent as a persuasive, powerful public speaker — a talent that no doubt had been polished by hours of listening to and repeating famous speeches during his boyhood.

The year 1828 was a momentous one for Johnson. He and Eliza had their first child, a girl they named Martha. It was also the year Johnson won his first public office, launching a lifetime of political activity. He did not carry on a political campaign; indeed, his election was more in the nature of a sneak attack.

A group of friends who agreed with Johnson's vigorous Democratic views decided to run him, McDannel, Lincoln, and a few others for positions on the town council, or board of aldermen. But, because the upper-class landowners had run the council since the founding of the town, Johnson's supporters decided to keep secret his candidacy and that of the others until the last minute. This would prevent the established local politicians from mounting an attack against the upstart tailor and his friends.

On the day of the election, Johnson's backers showed up at the polls and made speeches to the arriving voters. Their surprise strategy was successful. To the outrage of the town aristocrats, who grumbled about "the impudence and insolence of the laboring class," Johnson and the others were elected.

Johnson served as a Greeneville alderman for two terms of one year each. Even his opponents had to admit that he was efficient and honest. He also seized every opportunity to praise the working class and to promote the idea of "popular democracy," or participation in the government by all the people. This fundamental belief in the importance of the common man was the foundation of his entire political career.

Unfortunately, although Johnson's straightforward pride in his origins was admirable, it was accompanied by a deep distrust of anyone from a more cultivated or well-to-do background. And he felt sensitive and defensive about his own poverty and lack of a formal education. These traits made it difficult for him to mingle and work comfortably with many of the polished politicians he was to encounter in the future.

New Home, New Shop, New Office

In 1830, he and Eliza had their second child, a boy they named Charles. The room behind the tailor shop was now much too small for the growing family. Furthermore, Johnson desperately wanted his children to grow up in a home he owned, not in a rented cabin. Then, in 1831, he heard from his friend Lincoln of a small piece of property for sale near the courthouse. Although it took nearly all of their savings, the Johnsons bought the property, which included a house and a lot. Now, for the first time in his life, Andrew Johnson owned a home. Later, when a small building elsewhere in town came up for sale, Johnson decided it would make a perfect tailor shop. After buying it, he and his friends raised the building up onto logs and rolled it to the new lot.

By now, Johnson's tailoring business was thriving. He needed help, so he obtained some apprentices—something he might have found difficult to imagine when he was an apprentice himself, just a few years before. Because he had not lost his love of listening and learning while he worked, he hired schoolboys to come in and read to him and his workers. If he was unable to find a boy, he read aloud himself while sewing. "The moment the needle passed through the cloth," a friend later recalled, "his eye would return to the book."

Also in 1830, Johnson won a significant honor: he was elected mayor of Greeneville. In 1831, at the age of 23, he began his new duties. He had many supporters among the town's growing number of working-class voters, and he was re-elected twice, for a total of three terms as mayor. This was quite a triumph for the poor, unschooled young man who had been almost a beggar just a few years earlier.

Johnson had now become a person of considerable importance in his adopted hometown. In 1832, he was even made a trustee of the Rhea Academy, Eliza's old school—yet he had never attended school in his life! His growing self-confidence began to echo what his friends were telling him: that he had a future in politics outside Greeneville.

STATE LEGISLATURE

Johnson's second daughter, Mary, was born in 1832, and his second son, Robert, was born in 1834. But in spite of the mounting expenses of his growing family, Johnson continued to do well in his tailoring business. He was doing so well in fact, that by 1835 he was willing to take some time away from work in order to try for a new political goal. He hoped to be elected to the Tennessee state legislature in Nashville as a representative of Greene and Washington counties.

It was clear that Johnson would have to campaign hard to win this election. His opponent was Major Matthew Stephenson, a popular Whig and an experienced politician. Johnson decided to capitalize on his skills at speech-making. To draw attention – and votes – he challenged Stephenson to a series of public debates. He and his friend, Sam Milligan, prepared for the debates by digging through piles of newspaper clippings for records of Stephenson's statements and actions.

When the two met face to face at the first debate, Stephenson was lofty, polished, and rather pompous in manner. But the stuffing soon trickled out of him when Johnson took the floor. In a hard-hitting speech that pointed out every one of Stephenson's flaws in logic and inconsistent actions, Johnson reduced his opponent to a laughingstock. He also made a powerful personal appeal to his listeners to side with him against wealthy aristocrats who were committed only to protecting their own interests.

Each debate had the same result. And the voters among the working class rallied behind their spokesman. On election day, Johnson won by a small margin. Leaving Eliza in charge of the family and the business, he set off for the state legislature in Nashville.

A Union Man

One of the most important political issues of the day concerned states' rights. In 1787, the Constitution had bound the states together into the United States, but it did not spell out the exact nature of the relationship that held them together. Some leaders were in favor of a strong central government that would have greater power than the individual state governments. Other leaders believed that the states should have the right to act independently on most matters.

Those who favored a strong central, or federal, government were sometimes called Union men, because they believed the Union of the states was more important than the individual states themselves. Their opponents were called states' rights men. Every politician in the 1830s had to take a stand on one side or the other of this explosive issue.

Like his hero Andrew Jackson, Johnson was a Union man. He did not think that the states had the right to overrule the central government. He spoke out against a plan in South Carolina to nullify, or cancel, a federal law that was opposed by some state leaders. At the same time, however, he did not believe that the federal government should meddle unnecessarily in state or local matters. He felt that too much government was worse than no government at all. "There are no good laws," he is reported to have said, "but such as repeal other laws."

Opinions and Setbacks

Although he was a newcomer in the Tennessee state legislature, Johnson saw no reason why he should not stand up and speak his mind when he felt like it—indeed, this trait remained with him all his life. It caused him trouble at the beginning of his very first legislative session. Someone proposed a bill calling for a minister to open each session with a prayer. Johnson felt that the prayer bill was wrong, and he decided to say so.

Johnson made no secret of his feelings about religion. He read the Bible and quoted from it often, and he spoke of his belief in God. But, although he sometimes attended Methodist services with Eliza, he never belonged to a church. From time to time he attended the services of various denominations, and he approved and disapproved of different features of each faith.

However, he believed that, as far as government was concerned, church and state must remain separate in order to ensure equal religious freedom to all. So, despite warnings from more politically experienced friends, he made a speech against the prayer bill. The speech was not well received. It provided his enemies, who called him irreligious and anti-Christian, with ammunition to use against him in future campaigns.

Johnson spoke up freely on other matters, too. He had promised the people who voted for him that he would work to keep taxes low. Now other legislators wanted to raise the state debt by several million dollars in order to pay for a system of new roads throughout the state. Although the roads would benefit Johnson's two-county district, he opposed the plan. He called the scheme a "fraud" and predicted that unscrupulous operators would waste or make off with the state funds.

Johnson's stand against the roads was not very popular with the voters, as he discovered when he ran for re-election in 1837. He was voted out, and a Whig candidate who urged lavish spending of state funds was voted in. Johnson returned to tailoring.

The Voter's Choice Again

By 1839, Johnson's prediction about the road-building scheme had come true. Roads had been started, only to be left half-finished when swindlers made off with huge profits and the public funds ran out. The disgusted voters returned Johnson to office for the 1839–1841 legislative term.

As a state representative, Johnson took a big political step forward during the 1840 presidential campaign. He stumped the state (the term comes from the old-fashioned practice of making political speeches from atop a tree stump), leading rallies and making fiery speeches, on behalf of the Democratic presidential candidate, Martin Van Buren. He adopted as his slogan an expression long used by drovers, or wagon drivers, when helping each other pull their wagons out of holes in the road: "Stand hand in hand, shoulder to shoulder, foot to foot, and make a long pull, a strong pull, and all pull together!"

As Johnson's reputation for forceful oratory spread, his speeches began to draw huge crowds. In some towns, Johnson debated political issues with local Whigs, and these lively occasions made colorful reading in the newspapers. In other towns, the Whigs refused to debate with Johnson, and this too made news. Among the prominent state Whigs whom Johnson confronted during this speech-making tour were Thomas Nelson, an attorney, and William Brownlow, a newspaper editor. These two men were Johnson's political opponents in 1840; he did not know then that they were destined to be both his allies and his enemies in the future.

When the presidential election rolled around, Van Buren lost to William Henry Harrison in Tennessee. Nevertheless, Johnson had won statewide fame. In 1841, he was elected by a comfortable margin to the Tennessee Senate, the upper house of the state legislature; his friend, Sam Milligan, was voted into Johnson's former seat in the Tennessee House of Representatives.

STATE SENATOR

During his two-year term as state senator, Johnson took stands on two issues. One was a matter of local politics that was of no interest outside the region and was quickly forgotten, even by Tennesseans. The other concerned the growing conflict over slavery, an issue that would tear the nation apart in less than two decades.

Frankland

The local issue concerned the mountain people of East Tennessee. Most of them were small farmers and backwoodsmen, with few or no slaves and little concern for industry and business. Johnson felt that the needs and interests of these people were different from those of other Tennesseans. In fact, the mountain people of East Tennessee had more in common with those who lived in the adjoining mountain and backwoods regions of Virginia, North Carolina, and Georgia.

After touring the mountain district and listening to the people's complaints about the way the state was run, Johnson revived an old plan to create a new state from these backwoods regions. He proposed a bill in the state legislature to create a new state in the mountain region to be called Frankland. Although the bill was passed by the Tennessee Senate, it was not passed by the House of Representatives. The idea died and was not revived.

The Three-Fifths Rule

The second issue that occupied Johnson's attention during his term as a state senator concerned the increasingly troublesome problem of slavery. Across the nation, a passionate war of words was being waged between the abolitionists, who wanted to outlaw slavery, and the slaveowners of the South, who felt that slavery was vital to their way of life and wanted to see it spread into the new states of the West. In the 1840s and 1850s, this war would go beyond words, as both sides turned to acts of violence to make their points.

Like most southerners, Johnson accepted slavery as a fact of life. Eventually, he owned 10 slaves, and he believed that it was acceptable to consider them as just a form of property. But he came to feel that slavery was economically unjust, because it allowed the owners of the great plantations to prosper, while the small farmers who did not own slaves had to work hard just to survive. Always a supporter of the free working man, Johnson felt that large holdings of slaves, like large holdings of land, gave the wealthy too much power.

Johnson was further troubled by doubts about the morality of slavery. Unlike many southerners, he readily admitted that slavery could be cruel and inhumane. He did not join the abolitionists, however, and he did not really believe that black and white people could live together as free equals. He also shared the fears of many farmers and laborers that, if slavery were abolished, hordes of liberated slaves would compete with the working man for every job, making it impossible for many whites to earn a living. But he began to hope that, in time, the slave states would abandon slavery one by one.

In Tennessee, slaves even brought political power to their owners. Although slaves could not vote, a strange twist of the law said that each black person must be counted as three-fifths of a white person for the purpose of establishing the population of a district. Because the number of government representatives for each district was based on population, this meant that districts with large slave populations had more representatives in the state legislature than districts populated by free men. For example, if two districts had 5,000 whites each, but slaveholders in one district owned 15,000 slaves and the other district had no slaves, the slave-owning district would be credited with a population of 14,000. As a result, the slave-owning district might have five or six seats in the state legislature, while the other district had only two, even though they had the same number of voters.

Johnson thought that this system was unfair to the tradesmen and small farmers who did not own large numbers of slaves. He fought to have the law changed, but he was defeated. From that time on, the slaveowners of Tennessee and elsewhere in the South, even those who were members of his own Democratic Party, viewed Andrew Johnson as their enemy. For the moment, however, he did not care. He had proved that he could survive in the tough world of frontier state politics. Now he was ready for the next step.

Chapter 4

The Tennessee Tailor in Washington

In 1842 Johnson felt he was ready to represent the people of Tennessee in the nation's capital. He announced that he was running for a seat in the U.S. House of Representatives. This news was cheered by his admirers among the working-class Democrats.

However, the wealthy, upper-class Democrats of the area were not so pleased. They felt that Johnson did not have their best interests at heart — and they were right. They then united with local Whigs to support Colonel John Aiken against Johnson. But after a series of spirited debates, Johnson won the election. When the next session of Congress convened, in 1843, Congressman Johnson reported for duty in Washington, D.C.

As was the custom for most families of politicians at that time, Eliza and the four Johnson children remained home in Greeneville. Johnson rented a room in a boardinghouse near Capitol Hill and set about exploring the capital. Greeneville and Raleigh, the two towns in which Johnson had spent most of his life, each had a population of about 1,000 people. Washington's population was about 40,000.

Although it had muddy streets and many vacant, weed-grown lots, Washington also gave promise of grandeur to come in its new public buildings and broad avenues. But what Johnson liked best about the city was the Library of Congress. He spent much of his spare time there reading scores of books, everything from Aesop's *Fables* to biographies of statesmen such as Thomas Jefferson.

Perhaps the furor over his antiprayer speech had taught Andrew Johnson to start out cautiously in a new role. At any rate, he did what was expected of a new, junior congressman—he watched, listened, learned, and kept his mouth shut. Near the end of his first season in the House, he made his first speech. His hero, Tennessean Andrew Jackson, years earlier had been fined $1,000 for putting New Orleans under martial law during the War of 1812. Now an old man, Jackson was a war hero and a former President. A motion had been made to cancel the fine and repay Jackson the $1,000. Johnson made his congressional debut with a speech in support of this motion, which was passed.

A SENATOR OF PRINCIPLE

Before long, Johnson was speaking up on more controversial issues. He began making a name for himself as an argumentative, strong-minded politician who went his own way and did not always follow his fellow Democrats or his fellow southerners. He demonstrated this independent thinking in a notorious incident during his first term.

The "Gag Rule"

At the time, Congress had what was called the "gag rule." This rule prevented the legislature from hearing any proposals for bills that called for the abolition of slavery. The nation's lawmakers had learned that because this issue provoked such an uproar in Congress, no bill connected with abolition had any chance of being discussed and considered. Therefore, any congressman who tried to present such a bill was automatically voted out of order and the bill was not read. Because the rule silenced, or gagged, the abolitionists in Congress, it was a favorite of southern legislators.

At first, Johnson supported the gag rule, along with other southerners. John Quincy Adams of Massachusetts, a former President who was now a congressman, favored abolition and was the chief opponent of the gag rule. One day in Massachusetts, Adams claimed that if slavery could be abolished only by war, then war must come. Soon after, in the House, Johnson turned to the old legislator and said that, by advocating war, Adams was violating the Constitution. Adams ignored Johnson's taunt—but he wrote in his private diary that young Johnson of Tennessee had a sharp wit.

Johnson took a different stand, however, when a congressional crisis arose over the gag rule. Joshua Giddings, a northern abolitionist congressman, arose to present a bill. Either Giddings did not tell the Congress in advance that it concerned abolition, or—as he later claimed—he did tell the Congress but other congressmen were making so much noise that no one heard him. As a result, when he came to the portion of the bill that dealt with abolition, he was shouted down by angry southern congressmen.

An argument arose over whether Giddings had presented the bill unfairly. Giddings asked for permission to speak for himself. Johnson was among those who voted in favor of letting him speak to clear the air. He was the only southern congressman to do so. His enemies gleefully pounced upon this as proof that he was a traitor to the South, maybe even an abolitionist at heart. In truth, he was only acting by what he

Johnson and the Know-Nothings

During the 1840s, a new political party arose to challenge the two-party system of the Democrats and Whigs. This new party flourished for a few years before disintegrating at the end of the 1850s. Its short-lived power was based on fear and hatred of foreigners, especially immigrants who were Roman Catholics.

The party was originally a secret society, like the Freemasons and other lodges. It was called the Order of the Star Spangled Banner, and its members were united in their dislike of "foreign" influences in America. During the mid-19th century, immigration from European nations to the United States increased, and large cities such as Boston, New York, and Philadelphia began to have whole districts where these immigrants lived—and voted.

Many of the immigrants, especially the Irish and some of the Germans, were Catholics. Some people believed that, through them, the Roman Catholic Church could exercise a secret and sinister power in the United States. After the 1830s, labor disputes and ethnic riots in some cities further fueled the fear of foreigners.

Members of the Order of the Star Spangled Banner used secret handshakes, passwords, and rituals to create their own feeling of hidden power. To preserve the secrecy of the society, they were supposed to answer "I know nothing" whenever they were asked about the group or its meetings. When, in the late 1840s, the society changed its name to the American Party and became active in politics, it quickly was given the nickname "The Know-Nothing Party."

No one could become a member of the American Party who was not born or raised a Protestant or who was married to a Catholic. One of the party's written rules asked members: "Are you willing to use your influence and vote for native-born American citizens for all offices of honor, trust, and profit in the gift of the people, to the exclusion of all foreigners and aliens, and Roman Catholics in particular, and without regard to party predilection?"

Like Abraham Lincoln and many other free-thinking leaders, Johnson despised the Know-Nothings. He felt that they stood for prejudice, bigotry, and intolerance. He also felt that they supported the cruel class distinctions he had fought against as a poor boy and had been fighting against ever since. On a number of occasions, Johnson spoke out against Know-Nothing, or American, candidates. This earned him more enemies among the Whigs, who shared some Know-Nothing beliefs and sometimes supported Know-Nothing candidates.

In addition, Johnson was fundamentally tolerant toward all religions, and he hated religious intolerance. He made himself unpopular with the anti-Catholic forces when he said that he admired the equality of worship in the Catholic Church. In Catholic churches, he

pointed out, people sat in pews on a first-
come, first-served basis, whereas it was the
policy of most Protestant churches of the
time to reserve the best pews for the wealthy
families. This, for Johnson, was a mark in favor of the Catholics.

The high tide of Know-Nothing power
came in 1854, when American Party candidates won governorships and congressional
seats in a number of states. In the following
years, however, the party members could not
agree on the issue of slavery versus abolition.
Some of them joined the Whigs; later, the
Whig-based Republican Party absorbed many
Know-Nothings and finally swallowed up the
American Party entirely in the late 1850s. By
the time of the Civil War, the American Party
was all but extinct.

saw as the simple rules of justice. Once he had decided what
was right and what was wrong, he refused to back down to
please anyone.

As the presidential election of 1844 approached, Johnson opposed those Democrats who wanted James Polk, a
former governor of Tennessee, as the party's candidate. This
did not make Johnson popular with powerful Democrats, but
once Polk was nominated, Johnson loyally went along with
the party's choice. He made speeches for Polk in his home
district, where his old debating enemy, Thomas Nelson, was
making speeches for Henry Clay, the Whig candidate. Polk
won the presidency, and Johnson felt he had a good chance
of being re-elected to his congressional seat.

Parson Brownlow

Johnson's opponent in the 1844 congressional election was William Brownlow, a Whig newspaper editor who was sometimes called Parson Brownlow because he had been a preacher. He and Johnson waged a vicious battle for votes. Brownlow, known as the "fighting parson" for his aggressive, name-calling style of preaching and politicking, announced in his paper that Johnson was "a common and public liar, an impious infidel and an unmitigated villain."

Things went downhill from there, with both candidates slinging mud at each other for all they were worth. But at the end of the fight, Johnson emerged the victor, winning the election by an even greater margin than two years before. He returned to Washington in triumph, but he had made a bitter enemy in Parson Brownlow.

SECOND TERM

During his second term as a congressman, Johnson was as much a family man as he was a politician. He brought his 18-year-old daughter Martha to the capital and enrolled her in Mrs. English's Seminary for Young Ladies. On weekends, she visited her father, acted as his secretary and hostess, and sometimes paid social calls on President Polk in the White House.

Johnson frequently excused himself from these visits, because he and Polk did not get along well. Johnson was angry because Polk did not accept any of his recommendations to award government jobs to Johnson's friends and supporters. In turn, the President expected Democratic congressmen to support him loyally, but Johnson did not hide the fact that he disagreed with some of Polk's ideas. He did, however, support the President in one of his most unpopular acts, the war against Mexico for the territories of California and the American Southwest.

The Homestead Bill

Johnson's second term saw the introduction of one of his most cherished projects, the Homestead Bill. He believed that the small farmers and laborers of the working class were the backbone of America, and he felt that such people should have a chance to own land of their own. He proposed a bill that would grant 160 acres of government-owned land in the western territories to anyone who would homestead it, or live and work on it for five years.

As Johnson pointed out in speech after speech, the government owned 480 acres of land in the territories west of the Mississippi River for every voter in the United States. Giving this land to settlers who were willing to work hard and make it productive would not only create a self-supporting farming class but would also develop huge tracts of land that were lying empty and useless.

Powerful landowners in the South opposed the bill. They feared that, as settlers and farmers grew more numerous in the western territories, new states would be made out of these territories. The new states would probably be free states, not slave states, and the South would be outnumbered in Congress.

As a result of this opposition, Johnson was not able to get the Homestead Bill passed by Congress. He did not give up, however; he returned to the idea time and time again. Although the Homestead Bill was not passed until many years later, during Lincoln's presidency, Johnson deserves much of the credit for making public land available to the poor, land-hungry settlers who peopled the West.

FIGHTING TO HOLD ON

Johnson was re-elected four times to the U.S. House of Representatives. He thus served a total of five congressional terms in a row from 1843 to 1853. As time went on, however, opposition to him gained strength. President Polk made no secret of the fact that he would like to see another Tennessee Democrat take Johnson's place in Congress. Johnson was unpopular with some people in the federal government because he bluntly spoke his mind about abuses of power. He even "blew the whistle" on a congressman who was making a profit by illegally selling government property.

Such forthright honesty may be admired by the taxpayers, but it does not make a politician popular with his colleagues, many of whom were united against Johnson. And southern slaveowners continued to fear that he was too favorable to antislavery measures.

At a time when most of the nation's leaders were well-educated lawyers, professional men, or military officers, Johnson's "down-home" manners, rustic speech, and outspoken pride in his humble origins annoyed many congressmen. Some of them even referred to him scornfully as "the bound-boy of Raleigh," taunting him with his early years as an apprentice.

Although he sometimes reacted with harsh words of his own, Johnson believed that facts and honesty were more important than manners, style, or grammar. This behavior, of course, only endeared him more to the rural and small-town tradesmen, farmers, and mountaineers who were his biggest backers.

Once, on the floor of the House, Johnson spoke sharply to Representative Jefferson Davis of Mississippi about class distinctions. He and Davis were debating the need to add costly experts in military engineering to the staff of the U.S.

*The 1840s were busy and prosperous years for Congressman
Andrew Johnson. His blunt manners and his humble origins,
however, made him unpopular with many people in the nation's
capital.* (Library of Congress.)

Military Academy at West Point, New York. Johnson suggested that perhaps these experts were not needed. Referring to a fortress on the border between Texas and Mexico, Davis said haughtily, "Can a blacksmith or tailor construct the bastioned fieldworks opposite Matamoros?" Sensing an insult, Johnson leaped angrily to his feet and said, "I am a mechanic, and when a blow is struck on that class I will resent it." Further hot words were exchanged, and Davis joined the ranks of Johnson's enemies.

"Henrymandered" Out of Office

In subsequent re-elections to the House of Representatives, Johnson defeated Judge Oliver Temple, the Whig candidate, in 1846. In 1848 he defeated Colonel Nathaniel Taylor. In 1850, after two months of hours-long, mudslinging debates, he defeated Landon Haynes, a Democrat supported by the Whigs. Johnson returned to office for his fifth and final term as a congressman in a jubilant mood. He was so successful as a self-made politician that even when the two parties combined against him, they could not beat him.

Johnson was prospering in private life, too. Under the supervision of a foreman, his tailoring business brought in a steady income. In 1851 Johnson proudly moved his family into a gracious, high-ceilinged, two-story brick house. It stood on an acre of land, covered with the famous bluegrass of Kentucky and Tennessee and shaded by tall trees and an arbor of grape vines.

Martha, now home from Washington, helped her mother run the household. Charles, who had become a pharmacist, and Robert, who was studying law, also lived at home. Mary, the younger daughter, was married in 1852 to Dan Stover. That same year, Johnson and Eliza had their fifth and last child, a boy whom they named Andrew. Johnson spent a relaxing summer in the new house, with the baby and his family around him. But he was less happy with the political situation.

For five terms the Whigs had not been able to beat Johnson at the polls. But in 1850 the Whigs gained power in the Tennessee state legislature. They used this power to bring Johnson down.

A Whig named Gustavus Henry, a descendant of Patrick Henry, the famous Virginian of Revolutionary War days, pushed a bill through the Tennessee legislature to reorganize the voting districts of the state. Greene County, Johnson's home base, was detached from the surrounding district and attached to a district with a large majority of Whigs. This strategy was called "gerrymandering," after Elbridge Gerry, a governor of Massachusetts, who in 1812 had manipulated votes in his states by creating a new district that happened to be shaped like a salamander.

Johnson, however, disgustedly referred to the reorganization of his district as "Henrymandering," because it was Gustavus Henry who was responsible for the change. "The Whigs have cheated me out of Congress," Johnson complained. "They have torn the county of Greene from its sister counties, and attached it to a lot of foreign counties." To the dismay of the Whigs, however, this underhanded strategy soon backfired on them in a most dramatic way.

Chapter 5
Governor and Senator

The Tennessee Whigs who had gerrymandered Johnson out of his congressional seat in Washington soon had to deal with him much closer to home. When the Whig governor of Tennessee, W. B. Campbell, announced that he was retiring and would not run for re-election, Johnson let it be known that he would be willing to run as the Democratic candidate. Party bosses among the Democrats were unwilling to nominate the maverick Johnson. However, when they were overruled by delegates to the state convention, many of whom were farmers or mountaineers, Johnson received the Democratic nomination.

STATE MATTERS

Johnson was deeply satisfied with the candidate who the Whigs nominated for governor. He was Gustavus Henry, the man who had designed the state redistricting that had cost Johnson his congressional seat. Johnson made no secret of the fact that he hoped to give Henry a sound beating at the polls for personal as well as political reasons.

Clipping the Eagle's Wings

Henry was a gifted public speaker who was sometimes called "the Eagle Orator of the South." He was known for his fine phrases and smooth, rolling voice. But in Johnson he came up against a tough, no-holds-barred stump speaker who, as one newspaper reporter put it, "tore big wounds and left something behind to fester." After a few debates, Johnson's backers congratulated themselves that he had "clipped the wings" of the Eagle Orator. And Henry reportedly admitted to a friend, "I have never met so powerful a speaker as Andrew Johnson."

The election was close, but the new governor who took office in Nashville in October of 1853 was Andrew Johnson. As the state did not yet have a governor's mansion, he lived in a hotel room. His inauguration was simple and unpretentious. Instead of a big, expensive parade, he merely walked from his hotel to the capitol building, where he delivered a short speech about his belief that government should represent the common people as well as the wealthy and powerful. Then he settled down to the work of governing the state.

Johnson studied local issues and politics carefully and was a good governor. His most important action was to promote the idea of free education, to be paid for by increased taxes. His favorite project, though, was the purchase of The Hermitage, Andrew Jackson's home near Nashville, which was turned into a state-owned museum. Johnson also formed plans to reform the state's railway, prison, and banking systems, and he established state agricultural fairs and a state library. But Johnson was governor in difficult times.

Johnson Versus Gentry

The conflict between the Whigs (and Know-Nothings) on the one hand and the Democrats on the other was so severe in Tennessee that the legislature could hardly bring itself to agree on anything. More than 100 ballots were needed before the state senators could agree on a clerk for the Senate. Larger, more important matters roused still more controversy. Rivalry between the parties increased as the 1855 election for governor approached.

Tennessee Whigs, hoping to defeat Johnson, joined forces with the Know-Nothings to nominate Meredith Gentry as their candidate for governor. The campaign was bitter and very personal. With the help of Whigs such as Parson Brownlow and Thomas Nelson, Johnson's old debating opponents, Gentry raked up or manufactured many unsavory accusations about Governor Johnson: that he was a drunkard, that he was an abolitionist, that he was a man of loose morals. On his side, Johnson tore into Gentry and the Know-Nothings as cowards and "secret enemies" of the United States.

The debate sometimes escalated to threats of violence. On one occasion, when he was scheduled to make a speech in a community with many Know-Nothings, Johnson was warned that he would not leave the lecture hall alive. But he showed up on time, walked to the front of the room, laid a pistol on the speaker's table, and coolly said to the crowd, "I have been informed that part of the business to be transacted on the present occasion is the assassination of the individual who now has the honor of addressing you. If any man has come here tonight for that purpose, I do not say to him, let him speak, but let him shoot." Men in the crowd stirred and muttered uneasily, but they could not meet Johnson's steady gaze. He made his speech and left the hall with no further trouble.

After a nerve-wracking campaign, Johnson defeated Gentry. But in that election year around the country the Know-Nothings did gain temporary control of some of the border states between the South and the North, including Maryland and Kentucky. However, their power was broken in Tennessee, where Johnson served as governor until 1857.

WASHINGTON AGAIN

The mid-1850s were eventful years for Johnson in personal ways, too. His older daughter, Martha, was married in 1854 to David T. Patterson, a lawyer who was to become a senator years later. That same year, his mother-in-law died; his own mother died a year or two later.

In the spring of 1856, Johnson narrowly escaped death when his hotel in Nashville caught fire. He rescued a woman in a nearby room who was trapped by the flames, but all of his papers and other possessions were destroyed. Less than a year later, while returning from Washington, he was badly injured in a serious train accident. Despite a crushed arm, he recovered quickly enough to participate in another political campaign, this one designed to take him back to the nation's capital.

Buchanan for President

During the presidential campaign of 1856, Johnson had stumped heartily throughout Tennessee for the Democratic candidate, James Buchanan, even though he did not think much of the man or his politics. But Johnson knew that he needed to have Democratic party leaders behind him as never before if he hoped to achieve his new ambition: to become a United States senator.

At that time, U.S. senators were elected by the members of the state legislature instead of by a vote of the people. In order for Johnson to become a senator in 1857, two things had to happen. First, a lot of Democrats had to win seats in the Tennessee legislature; second, they had to be willing to support Johnson. Johnson figured that the best way to make sure both of these things happened was to work for a sweeping Democratic victory in the 1856 election. If he helped to get the Democratic candidate elected to the White House, the local Democrats would be more or less forced to back him against the Whigs for senator.

So Johnson turned his considerable speech-making skills to the service of Buchanan. He started things off with a three-hour speech in Nashville, which was heard by the biggest crowd he had ever addressed. He then followed this with stirring speeches all over the rest of the state. Buchanan was elected President—with the largest Democratic plurality in Tennessee since Andrew Jackson last ran for President more than 20 years before.

In the state elections the following August, Democrats dominated both houses of the Tennessee legislature. And in October of 1857, the Democrats in the legislature voted unanimously to send Johnson to Washington that winter as their new senator.

Johnson turned the office of governor over to Isham Harris, not knowing how soon he and Harris were to become enemies divided by war. As he set off for Washington, Johnson announced, "I have reached the summit of my ambition." But even he, an ambitious man, could not have guessed how much higher he was to rise—or how quickly he would fall.

STRIFE AND SECESSION

Johnson's term as a U.S. senator started off smoothly enough. He immediately revived his cherished Homestead Bill and began efforts to get it passed by the Senate. He also maintained that government funds ought to be spent cautiously and economically. And he generally went along with his fellow senators from the South in opposing antislavery legislation and urging stronger enforcement of the Fugitive Slave Law, which required that runaway slaves be returned to their masters.

However, Johnson also crossed swords with members of the government, including his own party's President. When

Buchanan vetoed the Homestead Bill, shattering Johnson's hopes of seeing it become law, Johnson accused him of favoring the slaveowning aristocrats of the South over the free working class. And he had more angry words with Jefferson Davis of Mississippi, now a senator and the leader of the Democrats of the Deep South. Johnson accused Davis of working harder to advance his own career than to protect the people. Davis had never liked Johnson, and this remark did not improve their relationship.

Conflict Between North and South

The late 1850s were a time of great unease and strife in Washington and throughout the land. The growing conflict between the slaveowners of the South and the abolitionists of the North was beginning to tear the nation apart.

Slavery had been a problem in the United States almost since the nation's birth. Some of the Founding Fathers, such as Thomas Jefferson, agonized over the question of whether to prohibit slavery in the new country. But the southern states, whose economy was based on slave labor and plantation agriculture, had threatened not to join the Union if slavery were banned. So, from the very beginning, the seeds of division were planted.

As the antislavery movement gained strength in the mid-19th century, northern abolitionists began to demand that the slaves be set free. But the issue that really brought the simmering conflict to a boil was not the existence of slavery in the southern states, where it was firmly entrenched. Rather, the crucial issue concerned the spread of slavery to new states and territories in the West.

Most people in the North insisted that the western territories must be admitted to the Union as free states. They wanted this partly for humanitarian reasons and partly because the economy of the North was based on small family farms, business, and industry. The northerners wanted their way of life, not the southern way of life, to spread westward. The South, on the other hand, insisted that some of the new states must be slave states so that the South would not be over-powered by a predominantly free-state Congress.

From the 1820s through the 1850s, a number of com-promises, trade-offs, and half-measures were proposed in an attempt to resolve this fundamental conflict between the North and the South. During Johnson's term in the Senate, these compromises began breaking down. Hatred of the abolitionists ran high in the South; some towns even offered cash boun-ties for their capture or assassination. Southern leaders and newspaper writers spoke openly of the possibility of seces-sion, or withdrawal from the Union. This was not the first time a dissatisfied state or region had threatened to secede from the Union, but this time the threat was much more seri-ous than ever before. People started to realize that a crisis was at hand.

Andrew Johnson, who believed with all his heart in the rightness of the Union that bound the states together, was deeply troubled. He was no friend of the Deep South, with its plantation aristocracy. But he certainly did not agree with the abolitionists, because he feared that freeing the slaves would cause untold grief for the poor white working class.

As a border state between the North and the South, some Tennesseans favored secession and some favored loyalty to the Union. Johnson stood in the middle; he called the two extreme points of view "run-mad abolitionists" and "red-hot disunionists." The only thing he was sure of was that seces-sion from the Union would not be a good thing for anyone. The United States must remain united.

The Campaign of 1860

Tension grew as the presidential election of 1860 approached. Quarrels between northern and southern Democrats split the party, which was unable to agree on a presidential candidate.

The only thing the Democrats did agree on was that President Buchanan was too ineffective to be nominated for a second term.

Some Democrats backed Senator Stephen Douglas of Illinois, who took the position that the people of the new western states should be allowed to vote on whether or not to permit slavery in each state. Other Democrats, mostly in the Deep South, backed Buchanan's Vice-President, John Breckinridge of Kentucky, who took the more extreme position that slavery was none of the government's business and could not be regulated by law because it was not prohibited by the Constitution. A few Democrats even felt that Johnson had a good chance, but his moderate position failed to attract enough delegates at the party's national convention. So the Democrats ended up fielding two presidential candidates, Douglas and Breckinridge.

Meanwhile, the Whig Party had dissolved. Many Whigs joined the new Republican Party, which was strongest in the North. The Republican candidate was Abraham Lincoln of Illinois. Lincoln's position on the burning issue of the day was not as simple as history has sometimes made it seem. He said many times that he was neither for slavery nor against it. He was firmly in favor of preserving the Union from the threat of secession by whatever means were necessary; keeping the nation together, not freeing the slaves, was his primary goal.

Over and over, Lincoln assured the South that, although he did not want to see slavery spread into the West, he had no intention of interfering with slavery in the states where it was already established. The southern leaders, however, did not believe that Lincoln would permit slavery to continue in their home states. They called him a "Black Republican" and vowed to secede if he were elected.

There was also a fourth candidate in the election of 1860.

Some former Whigs joined with the Know-Nothings of the rapidly dying American Party to nominate John Bell, who was Tennessee's other senator and no friend of Johnson's. But few people felt that Bell had any chance of winning.

The coming election put Johnson in a difficult position. Not only was he unable to win the nomination, but now he must decide which candidate to support in his home state. Bell was not worth considering. Lincoln's election, Johnson felt, would be a disaster, because it would lead to secession — and who knew what might happen then? The moderate views of Douglas were attractive; but as a northerner, Douglas could probably not get enough votes to carry Tennessee. So Johnson threw his rather halfhearted support behind Breckinridge. Once again he set off on a speech-making tour around the state.

Those Tennesseans who favored the South were mostly the big planters in the central and western parts of the state. Those who favored the North were mostly the small farmers and mountaineers of the eastern part of the state, Johnson's home territory. The campaign was difficult, with strong feelings on both sides, but Johnson left no one in doubt as to his own position.

The idea of secession was popular in the important Tennessee city of Memphis. When Johnson made a speech there, urging voters to elect Breckinridge, someone asked him, "Senator Johnson, what do you advise the South to do if Lincoln is elected?" Johnson was never one to veil his opinions with double-talk or half-truths, even when he knew they might not be well received. Without hesitation, he told his audience how he stood on the issue of secession. "As for myself," he replied firmly, "I shall stay inside the Union and there fight for southern rights. I advise all others to do the same." Unfortunately, Johnson's good advice was destined not to be followed.

Chapter 6
The War Years

The Democratic vote in the fall of 1860 was split between Breckinridge and Douglas. As a result, neither candidate could get enough votes to beat Lincoln, who also lacked a majority of popular votes. However, the Illinois Republican did receive enough votes in the electoral college to become the country's next President.

Johnson returned to Washington in December 1860, a few weeks after the presidential election, to take his seat in the new session of the Senate. The capital was filled with rumors, threats, and wild talk of secession and war. The uneasy mood was like the tense, charged atmosphere before a violent thunderstorm. The storm broke on December 18, when the grim-faced senators and congressmen of South Carolina declared their state's withdrawal from the Union. Amid cheers from the southerners who lined the galleries of the Senate, the South Carolina senators stalked from the chamber. Angry shouts came from the northerners on the floor. It was then that Andrew Johnson rose from his seat and made one of his finest—and most notorious—speeches.

"A ROPE OF SAND"

No one knew quite what to expect as Johnson rose to speak. The northerners regarded him as a southerner; they expected him to support South Carolina's actions. And the southerners knew that Johnson had spoken out against secession, although some of them hoped that he had changed his mind. But, as always, his opening words made everything clear: "I am opposed to secession," he announced.

When the uproar caused by this statement had died down a little, Johnson continued, his deep-set dark eyes flashing and his stern voice rising and falling dramatically. "No state has the right to secede from this Union without the consent of the other states. If the doctrine of secession is to be carried out upon the mere whim of a state, this government is at an end!" he cried. "It is no better than a rope of sand!"

Johnson went on to criticize the extremists of both North and South. His speech was interrupted often. Many southern senators called him a traitor to the South. Finally he burst out in anger, "Here is the issue: We are angry because Mr. Lincoln has been elected and we have not got our man. If we had got our man, we should not be against breaking up the Union, but as he *is* elected, we are breaking up the Union. Am I to be so great a coward," he demanded scornfully, knowing that no other word so touched the southern sense of honor, "as to retreat from duty?"

So many and so heated were the interruptions that Johnson was forced to wait until the next day to finish his speech. "Though I fought against Lincoln, I love my country," he declared. "I love the Constitution and swear that it and the Union shall be saved. . . . Senators, my blood, my existence I would give to save this Union!"

Johnson then ended his speech on a note of stirring patriotism, calling the Union and the Constitution "the last hope of human freedom." As he left the somber Senate chamber, the more hot-headed of his southern colleagues followed him down the street to his hotel, Kirkwood House, hurling insults at him and challenging him to duels. But Johnson ignored them and went his way.

Renegade Hero

Telegraph wires hummed as they carried Johnson's speech to newspapers across the country. Suddenly he found himself thrust into the limelight in both the South and the North.

The South reacted as might have been expected. Johnson's old enemy, Jefferson Davis of Mississippi, called him a "southern traitor." Texas Senator Lewis Wigfall called him a "renegade" and a "jackal." In southern cities—including Memphis and Nashville in Johnson's own Tennessee—jeering crowds dragged effigies, or stuffed dummies, of Johnson through the streets and then burned or hanged them. His life and the lives of his family were threatened. The ugly mood of many former friends and neighbors frightened Eliza and deeply saddened Johnson.

In the North, however, Johnson was the hero of the hour. He received thousands of requests for printed copies of his speech, hundreds of letters of praise, and scores of invitations to speak to clubs and political groups in northern cities. Even northerners who had been unenthusiastic about the Union were fired into patriotic zeal by his example. And many who had been willing to let the southern states depart without a fuss now began to say, with Johnson and Lincoln, "The Union must be preserved." In this way, perhaps, Johnson helped bring the North closer to war. If so, he would not have wanted it otherwise, for he surely believed that the Union was a cause worth fighting for.

THE CONFEDERACY

In early 1861, before Lincoln's inauguration as President, six other states followed South Carolina's lead and seceded. They were Mississippi, Georgia, Florida, Alabama, Louisiana, and Texas. They formed a government that they called the Confederate States of America, or the Confederacy, and elected Jefferson Davis as its president. Confederate leaders urged the other southern states to join them. And Johnson wondered: What would Tennessee do?

Isham Harris, who had succeeded Johnson as governor of Tennessee, made no secret of his support for the secessionists. He agreed to raise troops and taxes to support the Confederacy. But, to Johnson's relief, the state legislators voted to keep Tennessee in the Union. Harris was determined to join the Confederacy, however. He started organizing a referendum, or statewide vote of the people, and he was sure that the people would vote to secede. In Washington, Johnson made a Senate speech that passionately appealed to Tennessee to stay in the Union and to the South to call off its revolt.

"The Stars and Stripes, under which our fathers fought and bled and conquered, and achieved our rights and liberties, is trailed in the dust," he proclaimed, and he concluded, "Show me who has fired upon our flag, has given instructions to take our forts and our custom-houses, our arsenals, and our dockyards, and I will show you a traitor!" The Unionists leaped onto their chairs and cheered him, but his heart was heavy, for he feared that the South had gone too far to return now.

Two days later, Lincoln was inaugurated. A few weeks after that, Johnson received word that Tennessee's referendum was at hand. Secessionists threatened to kill him if he dared to enter the state, but he decided to go home anyway, to make a final appeal to his people to stay true to the Union.

Fort Sumter and War

In early April, as Johnson prepared for his journey to Tennessee, Confederate forces fired upon the Union troops who were manning Fort Sumter, located in the harbor of Charles-

The Confederates who fired on Fort Sumter, in the harbor of Charleston, South Carolina, in April of 1861 did not realize that they had fired the first shots in a four-year-long civil war that would be the country's bloodiest conflict ever. (Library of Congress.)

ton, South Carolina. President Lincoln had warned that he would not attack the South, but that he would respond with force to any southern act of aggression. Now he lived up to that warning. He sent out a call for volunteers to form a Union Army to attack the South. The Civil War begun.

Now that the conflict between the two regions had broken out into open warfare, Johnson, the southern senator who had sided with the North, was the object of special hatred in the South. On his way back to Tennessee, Johnson's train was traveling through Virginia at about the time that state declared its secession. Knowing he was on the train, angry crowds surrounded each station as the train pulled in, shouting that Johnson should be dragged off and hanged. When members of one mob broke into Johnson's car, he had to scuffle with them before they were thrown out.

These distressing incidents in Virginia gave Johnson some indication of what he could expect in Tennessee, where Governor Harris was urging the people to abandon the Union and stand by "our southern brothers." In areas where Confederate sympathies were strong, anyone who spoke in favor of the Union risked threats, beatings, or worse.

Nonetheless, Johnson went ahead, with the full support of his family, who worried for his safety (and theirs) but shared his pro-Union views. He made speeches throughout the state, sometimes with a revolver stuck into his pocket to quell possible violence. He had two surprising allies. His old Whig enemies, Thomas Nelson and Parson Brownlow, both strong Union men, spoke side by side with Johnson. All three men urged their audiences to forget the old divisions between Democrats and Whigs (now Republicans) and between northerners and southerners. For the good of the country as a whole, they pleaded, vote for the Union.

"A Fugitive from Tyranny"

Johnson's efforts could not turn the tide of rebellion. When the referendum was held, Tennessee voted to secede. Only in the eastern part of the state did a majority of the people vote to remain in the Union. Governor Harris then sent troops into East Tennessee to crush the pro-Union movement and announced that Tennessee was now part of the Confederate States of America. And Senator Andrew Johnson faced immediate arrest, possibly even assassination, as a traitor.

Johnson's family and friends begged him to flee, so he agreed to return to Washington. He left Greeneville under a poster stretched across the main street. It said, "Andrew Johnson, Traitor." As he crossed the Cumberland Gap into Kentucky, a Union state, Johnson said bitterly to the friends who had accompanied him, "Officers with warrants are hunting me down, but I am no fugitive—except a fugitive from tyranny."

The next year was a frustrating and anxious time for Johnson. He worried about his family, caught up in the turmoil of war. Eliza and young Andrew remained in Greeneville, safe in their home for the time being, but in constant fear of arrest by the Confederates. Martha's husband, David Patterson, had been imprisoned. Mary's husband, Dan Stover, was the object of a fierce manhunt. He was the leader of a group of Tennessee mountaineers who staged lightning-fast raids from Kentucky into Tennessee to destroy Confederate railroads and bridges. Charles and Robert Johnson also managed to escape to Kentucky. Charles was working as a doctor for the Union army and Robert was a colonel with a regiment of his own.

But Johnson remained in Washington, where he found himself in the peculiar position of being Congress' only southern legislator – and completely cut off from the state he was supposed to be representing. This made him a hero in the North. One New York newspaper called him "that staunch and fearless United States Senator." He was named one of seven members of a Joint Committee – that is, one with members from both the Senate and the House of Representatives – on the Conduct of the War. The purpose of the committee was to oversee and hurry along all the government departments and activities that contributed to the war effort.

Johnson's long hours of hard work on the committee earned him prestige and the respect of his colleagues. And a resolution, or motion, that he offered in Congress was adopted as the administration's official policy of war. It said that the purpose of the war was not to oppress or conquer the South, but "to defend and maintain the supremacy of the Constitution . . . and to preserve the Union, with all the dignity, equality, and rights of the several states unimpaired."

Johnson's chief activity as a senator was urging Lincoln to send Union forces into Tennessee. In the course of many long conversations, Johnson became first a reluctant admirer and finally a friend of the lanky Republican President. Although they were from different regions and different political parties, the two men had much in common. Both came from poor, working-class backgrounds, and both were self-educated, self-made men. More important, both believed with all their hearts that the southern states had no right to secede and that the Union must be preserved, even at the cost of war.

GOVERNOR AGAIN

In early 1862, Union forces won some crucial victories in western and central Tennessee. Although eastern Tennessee, Johnson's home, and parts of the rest of the state remained under Confederate control, the Confederate state government fled from the capital at Nashville. Lincoln then wanted to use Tennessee as an example of how a rebel state could be brought back into the Union. So he decided to establish a strong government in the Union-controlled territory at once, under the protection of the army. He asked Johnson to serve as military governor, and Johnson agreed.

Johnson thereupon exchanged his seat in the U.S. Senate for a military rank, that of brigadier general. His orders were to restore Union authority to those areas in Tennessee that had been seized by the Union army. Johnson served as military governor of Tennessee for two years, although many people in both the North and the South confidently expected that the war would be over within a few weeks or months.

When Johnson arrived in Nashville in March of 1862, he found that the state capital was practically a battlefield. Confederate troops ringed the city at a distance of less than 40 miles. The bloody Battle of Shiloh was fought southwest of the city on April 6 and 7.

Although the Union army controlled the Nashville area, the hearts of the people were for the South, and many of them voiced their hatred of the occupying northerners. Even the 20-year-old daughter of the owner of the hotel where Johnson was living in Nashville was brought before him on a charge of spitting on Union soldiers from the hotel porch and boasting that she would soon dance on Johnson's grave. Johnson managed a weary smile and dismissed the case, saying to his generals, "You mustn't mind these little rebels."

The military governorship was stern work. To quell Confederate sympathies, Johnson shut down newspapers that criticized the Union and even arrested preachers who spoke against the Union in church. He required all government workers to take an oath of loyalty to the Union and fired those who refused.

Johnson intervened in many cases to keep the army from being too severe in its punishment of Confederate sympathizers. For the most part, however, he maintained strict martial, or military, law, in which many common rights — such as the right of assembly and the right of free speech — were suspended. Some people later claimed that he had been too harsh, but most, including Lincoln, believed that he was a just governor, though a strict one.

The Siege of Nashville

Johnson worked day and night, often snatching a few hours' sleep on a couch in the capitol building, which was nicknamed Fort Johnson. He faced a desperate challenge in the summer, when the Confederate army came within eight miles of Nashville, cut off railroads and supply lines, and besieged the city for two months.

With food and medical supplies in short supply, the citizens of Nashville were eager to surrender to the Confederates, and even some of the Union officers hinted at that possibility. But Johnson was unwavering. "I am no military man," he said, "but anyone who talks of surrendering I will shoot."

Fortunately, the siege was lifted before such drastic steps became necessary. Johnson received much of the credit for saving the city. But Greeneville was in enemy hands, and Eliza and Andrew were turned out of the Johnson house, which became a Confederate barracks. Troops stationed there amused themselves by scrawling "Traitor to the South!" and "Shame on Old Andy!" on the walls.

By the end of the year, however, the Johnson family was reunited when Eliza, the children, and the grandchildren made their way through enemy lines to Nashville. The relief he felt at being able to protect his family allowed Johnson to carry on his grueling governorship with renewed energy. Sadly, though, Eliza's difficult journey had made her ill. She developed tuberculosis and had to spend much of her time in bed. At about the same time, Dan Stover, one of Johnson's sons-in-law, died of the same disease. Soon after, in early 1863, Johnson's son Charles died after a fall from his horse. Despite these private griefs, Johnson still worked for 14 hours or more each day.

As the war dragged on and Johnson doggedly persisted in his task of establishing an orderly government in troubled Tennessee, President Lincoln's respect and liking for this tough, capable, and loyal man increased. The two men kept in regular contact through telegrams and dispatches (messages carried by military couriers). Johnson's performance as military governor, and Lincoln's growing confidence in him, brought about a surprising new step in Johnson's career as the agonizing war drew toward a close.

Chapter 7
The National Union Party

Although today he is regarded as a hero and one of the greatest American Presidents, Lincoln was by no means popular with everyone during his lifetime. The southerners hated him, of course. Democrats who lived in the North, even those who approved of the war and were called War Democrats, disliked him because he was a Republican and had defeated their candidate, Stephen Douglas. The abolitionists among the Northern Republicans disliked him because he had been willing to tolerate slavery in the South if he could have prevented war by doing so.

Even many of the more moderate Republicans, the people who had supported Lincoln from the start, grew disillusioned with him when the war dragged on into a second, then a third, year. They felt that he should have chosen better generals, or taken more decisive action against the South, or done something—anything—to end the war. Lincoln's popularity declined drastically throughout 1862. In the fall of that year, hoping to win some of his critics to his side, he laid the groundwork for one of the acts for which he is most respected today: the Emancipation Proclamation.

JOHNSON AND EMANCIPATION

In the beginning of 1863, Lincoln issued a proclamation, or declaration, that freed all the slaves of states that were then in rebellion against the Union. In truth, however, this Emancipation Proclamation was more of a symbol than an actual freeing of the slaves. Most of the nation's slaves — some three million of them — were in the South, where the proclamation could not be enforced. The proclamation did not free the much smaller number of slaves in the border states, such as Maryland and Kentucky, that had remained loyal to the Union; nor did it free the slaves in the parts of those southern states that had been returned to Union control, such as regions of Louisiana and Virginia.

In the seceded states, however, the Emancipation Proclamation was rightly viewed as the death blow to slavery in America. Although he had avoided taking an abolitionist stand because he hoped to persuade the southern states to remain peaceful, President Lincoln believed slavery to be wrong.

Once he realized that the South was determined to continue the war, Lincoln saw no harm — and much good — in freeing the slaves. And he made it clear that the Emancipation Proclamation was just the beginning, that he expected slavery to be abolished everywhere in the land by an amendment to the Constitution (as it was, early in 1865, when Congress passed the 13th Amendment).

One state received special treatment in the Emancipation Proclamation. That state was Tennessee. Because Tennessee had formally seceded from the Union, it was among the states in which slavery would be outlawed by the proclamation. Johnson, however, convinced Lincoln to make an exception in the wording of the proclamation, allowing slavery to continue in Tennessee. The people of his divided state,

Johnson said, would be much more likely to favor a return to the Union if they were allowed to vote for themselves on the slavery issue, rather than having the decision forced upon them by a President whom most of them hated. After all, Johnson argued, not even all of the people who supported the Union were in favor of abolishing slavery. In Tennessee, and throughout the North, there were some who felt that, in issuing the Emancipation Proclamation, Lincoln had taken too much power upon himself. Slavery was doomed, however, and by now most people realized it. Johnson felt that the loyal Tennesseans would probably vote to abolish slavery if they were given the chance.

After much thought, Lincoln agreed. Johnson was doing a good job of governing Tennessee and had made all the necessary preparations to bring his state back into the United States as soon as a sufficient number of citizens swore the required oath of loyalty to the Union. So Lincoln trusted Johnson's judgment.

Finally, after two years of argument and debate, often interrupted by battles around Nashville, a state constitutional convention was held in February of 1865. A new state constitution was approved that outlawed slavery and cancelled the earlier act of secession. By this time, however, Johnson was no longer military governor of Tennessee. Lincoln had rewarded him for his loyalty by making him Vice-President of the United States.

A NEW POLITICAL PARTY

So unpopular had Lincoln become by 1864, the fourth year of the Civil War, that he feared he would not be re-elected in that year's presidential election. Hoping to drum up more backing, he and his supporters decided that it was necessary to do away with the old barriers between the Democratic and Republican parties. The so-called War Democrats of the North seemed now to have more in common with the Republicans than with the Democrats of the South. For that reason, the leading Republicans suggested the formation of a new political party. Called the National Union Party, or sometimes just the Union Party, it would bring together Republicans and War Democrats to back Lincoln for President.

Lincoln's Vice-President during his first term had been a Republican from Maine named Hannibal Hamlin. Hamlin's most noteworthy act as Vice-President had been to join the Union war effort. He served in the Coast Guard, where he was recognized for his good cooking but saw no action. Although he contributed nothing to Lincoln's presidency, he was a harmless, good-natured fellow who quite clearly expected to run for re-election with Lincoln in 1864. Unfortunately for Hamlin, Lincoln had other plans.

A New Vice-President

The national convention of the Union Party, at which the candidates for President and Vice-President would be nominated, was scheduled for June of 1864. As the convention drew nearer, Lincoln confided in some of his supporters that he had a new and very surprising idea about the vice-presidency.

At the time the National Union Party was formed, many people felt that it was really just the Republican Party under a new name, because Republicans far outnumbered Democrats on the party's rolls. But what if a Democrat were nominated to run for Vice-President with a Republican President? Surely that would convince the War Democrats that they were part of the Union Party, too.

Moreover, having a Vice-President from the South would show, as nothing else could, Lincoln's determination to bring the South back into the union of the states. It would show, in fact, that the South was still part of the United States, as Lincoln had claimed since the first secession was announced. In addition, northerners would remember Johnson's heroic stand in the Senate several years before and the praise lavished on him by newspapers as "the only loyal senator from the South." Finally, Lincoln himself had come to have the utmost confidence in this sturdy, plain-spoken southerner.

Only one thing made Lincoln hesitate. Rumors had reached his ears that Johnson had been extremely harsh — some said unnecessarily harsh — as military governor of Tennessee. To find out whether there was any truth in these rumors, Lincoln sent General Daniel Sickles, a trusted Union commander, to Nashville. Sickles, who had been retired from combat duty after he lost a leg at the battle of Gettysburg, was to investigate Johnson's treatment of the people of Tennessee. When Sickles reported to Lincoln that Johnson had acted fairly and had not abused his power, the President was satisfied. Later, some of Johnson's critics were to claim that a civilian, rather than a military man, would have been a fairer judge of Johnson's military government, but most historians today agree with Sickles' judgment.

After hearing Sickles' report, Lincoln made it clear that he wanted Johnson to run on the National Union ticket with him in the fall. Johnson was pleased and honored and hoped to win the nomination. He proclaimed his allegiance to the Union Party, although he was too busy preparing for Tennessee's constitutional convention to go to Washington and take part in the back-room meetings and negotiations that preceded the party convention. However, not everyone greeted Lincoln's decision favorably.

The Radicals and the "Rebel"

Among the Republicans in Congress was a group called the Radicals. This group was more extreme than other Republicans in their party's views and opinions ("radical" means "extreme" or "drastic"). These Radicals, most of whom were strict antisouthern abolitionists, wanted not so much to bring the Confederate states back into the Union as to crush the rebellion and then treat the South as a conquered enemy. They did not like the idea of the Union Party mixing Republicans with Democrats, and they did not like Lincoln. In fact, they had hoped to keep him from running for a second term. But even the most radical of the Radicals could not find another candidate with a good chance of winning, so they were forced to back Lincoln.

Johnson, however, was not so necessary, as the Radicals made clear when his name entered the discussion of possible Vice-Presidents. As a slaveowner, a southerner, and a former Democrat, he was totally unacceptable to the Radical Republicans. To them, the fact that Johnson was a southerner by birth far outweighed the sacrifices and dangers he had endured to prove his loyalty to the Union. Many Radicals thought of him as one of the "rebels" at heart, and an uneducated, common one at that.

"Can't we find a candidate for Vice-President of the United States without going down to one of those blasted rebel provinces to pick one up?" grumbled Thaddeus Stevens of Pennsylvania, the leader of the Radicals in the House of Representatives. But Lincoln countered firmly with statements such as "No man has a right to judge Andrew Johnson in any respect who has not suffered as much as and done as much as he for the Nation's sake."

Lincoln let it be known that he expected Johnson to be nominated at the party convention, and the Radicals were not yet strong enough to defy the President. But Stevens resented Lincoln's choice. In years to come, this powerful and angry old congressman would be Johnson's chief foe, a bitter and determined enemy.

A Convention in Baltimore

The national convention of the Union Party met in Baltimore on June 7, 1864. Lincoln was nominated immediately to run for re-election as the party's candidate for President. When the delegates turned their attention to nominating a candidate for Vice-President, things went less smoothly. Johnson was nominated (the nomination was seconded by Johnson's old enemy and now friend, Parson Brownlow, who represented Tennessee at the convention), but so were Hannibal Hamlin and Daniel Dickinson. Now the delegates would cast their votes.

In the first ballot, Johnson received 200 votes, Hamlin 150, and Dickinson 61. Because Johnson did not have a majority of the votes, other ballots followed. Seeing that Lincoln's favorite choice seemed likely to win, the delegates started to switch their votes to Johnson. In the end, he received all but 26 votes for the nomination and became the Union Party's candidate for Vice-President. Back home in Tennessee, however, where he received telegrams of congratulations from Brownlow and others, Johnson knew that the battle had only begun. Now he had to get elected.

THE CAMPAIGN OF 1864

The announcement of Johnson's candidacy for Vice-President brought a variety of responses. Pro-Unionists in the North and the border states, those who wanted to end the war and

The National Union Party was a short-lived union of Republicans and Democrats. In 1864, it nominated Republican Abraham Lincoln for re-election as President and Democrat Andrew Johnson for Vice-President. (Library of Congress.)

knit the North and South back together again, rejoiced. Radical Republicans were annoyed because everything that Lincoln did annoyed them and because they hated all southerners.

Some wealthy and aristocratic northerners, especially members of old, established families on the East Coast, were particularly dismayed that not one but both of the nation's two highest offices might be held by men from humble, uncultivated backgrounds. Lamented the *New York World,* "The age of statesmen is gone; the age of rail splitters and tailors, of buffoons, boors, and fanatics has succeeded, and the country is asked to consider the claims of two ignorant, boorish, third-rate backwoods lawyers for the highest stations in the government."

Abe and Andy

The Lincoln-Johnson ticket did offer opportunities for clever cartoonists to depict the two candidates in amusing and lively ways. Although he was a prosperous, successful lawyer at the time of his election to the presidency, Lincoln had been unable to escape the image of his early, impoverished years on the prairies of the Midwest, when he earned a reputation as a skilled axe-handler and splitter of fence rails. And Johnson, the tailor of Greeneville, was the first tradesman to aspire to high office. Both supporters and opponents of the two men played upon their backgrounds. Supporters hoped to arouse the pride of the working class; opponents hoped to arouse the scorn of the upper class.

Homespun images poured forth from the pens of artists and writers. Union Party campaign posters showed Abe, the rail-splitter, mending the broken fences between the North and the South. One cartoon that was widely reproduced showed tall, lanky Abe holding pieces of a torn map of the United States, while short, stocky Andy stitched at it with his tailor's tools, saying, "Take it quietly, Uncle Abe. I will draw it closer than ever and the good old Union will be mended."

But Lincoln's and Johnson's hopes of mending the "good old Union" seemed to recede almost out of reach during the summer and fall of 1864. The Union army suffered a series of stinging defeats by the Confederates, and the outcry against Lincoln's conduct of the war was renewed. In addition, because of the high cost of the war, the Union was close to running out of money—one more reason for Lincoln's leadership to be criticized.

A former Union general, George B. McClellan, was nominated to run for President on the Democratic ticket. As McClellan's campaign began to gather steam, Lincoln wrote in a private note in August that "it seems exceedingly probable that this administration will not be re-elected."

On the Campaign Trail

Johnson stayed in Tennessee during most of the campaign. He had work to do, preparing for the state constitutional convention. He also had to prepare to turn over the governorship to a successor who was to be elected, not appointed by military or presidential authority. But Johnson did campaign vigorously within his home state, even though political meetings in that hot-tempered year often ended in riots or fistfights as Radicals, Democrats, and Unionists tried to break up each others' gatherings. And many Tennesseans ignored the election entirely because they had not given up hope of a Confederate victory.

Declaring that he was too busy in Tennessee to go on a speech-making tour around the country, Johnson tried to help the campaign by writing scores of letters to newspapers and Union Party leaders in Ohio, Pennsylvania, New York, and other states. Finally, in September, at the pleading of party managers, Johnson did make one short trip into Indiana, where, in his stump orator's voice, he called for support of Lincoln and the Union.

Perhaps Johnson's most stirring and heartfelt campaign speech was the one he made from the steps of the Tennessee state capitol building on the night of October 24, after he had been cheered by a torchlight parade through the war-torn streets of Nashville. He referred to many of the insults and threats that he and his family had received during the years since the secession of the South. And he asked the crowd, "What crime have I committed to merit such treatment?"

As he spoke these words, the one-time runaway apprentice may have been thinking of a lifetime of snubs and harsh treatment by those who thought they were his "betters" simply because they were born to their good fortune while he had to work for his. If so, Johnson was soon to have a moment of victory over the snobs and aristocrats he disliked so intensely.

Fortune favored Lincoln and Johnson in the weeks before the election. The Union army won some important victories, and the South was on the run at last. There were some who began to say that the tide of war had finally turned in favor of the North, and that the South's resistance would soon be broken. Indeed, although no one could know it at the time, the South would be defeated and the war would be over less than six months after the election.

In this optimistic atmosphere, voters of the North went to the polls in November and elected Lincoln and Johnson President and Vice-President, respectively, for the coming four years. In both the popular vote and the electoral college vote, the rail-splitter from Illinois and the tailor from Tennessee carried the day. When news of the Lincoln-Johnson victory reached Nashville by telegraph, another torchlight parade was held in Johnson's honor.

However, those who had opposed the Union Party candidates were equally quick to show their displeasure. Johnson came in for another burst of peevish criticism in Democratic and Radical newspapers. One paper, the *New York World*, went so far as to publish the hope that Johnson would never become President through Lincoln's death, saying, "To think that one frail life stands between this insolent, clownish creature and the Presidency! May God bless and spare Abraham Lincoln!" The editors and readers of the *World* had no way of knowing how soon, or how tragically, the event they dreaded would occur.

Chapter 8

Reconstruction and the Republicans

The inauguration of President Abraham Lincoln and Vice-President Andrew Johnson was scheduled for March 4, 1865. But near the end of February Johnson was still in Nashville. For several reasons, he had not set out for Washington as he was expected to do.

For one thing, the strain of the campaign, on top of his two-year effort to hold a state constitutional convention, had exhausted the 56-year-old Vice-President-elect. In addition, he had fallen ill with a fever. But Johnson's biggest reason for lingering in Tennessee, where he had waged such a determined crusade to reclaim the state for the Union, was that he hated leaving a job unfinished.

Johnson felt that his work in Tennessee would not be complete until he had officially turned over the reins of state government to Parson Brownlow, who would be inaugurated as governor in March. So Johnson wrote to Lincoln asking to be excused from the inauguration ceremony and to the clerk of the Senate asking if he could receive the oath of office in a separate ceremony in Nashville.

Lincoln replied in a telegram that summed up his feelings and those of his Cabinet members: "While we fully appreciate your wish to remain in Tennessee until that state government shall be inaugurated, it is our unanimous conclusion that it is unsafe for you not to be here on the 4th of March. Be sure to be here by that time." By "unsafe," Lincoln meant that Johnson's absence would give the Radical Republicans and the Democrats an excuse to criticize the solidarity of the Union Party. This would make it more difficult for Lincoln and Johnson to control their opponents in the House of Representatives and the Senate.

The President feared that people would misinterpret Johnson's absence to mean that Johnson thought that Tennessee was more important than the Union. As events turned out, however, Lincoln may have wished that he had given Johnson permission to stay in Tennessee and miss the inauguration after all.

A MEMORABLE INAUGURATION

When he read Lincoln's telegram, Johnson wearily agreed to take the next train for Washington. He felt too ill to stop and make speeches at cities and towns along his route, although he received many invitations to do so. After he arrived in Washington on March 1 and settled in at Kirkwood House, he spent the next several days having his picture taken, being visited by friends and congressmen, and trying to rest.

One important ceremony during this time was Johnson's formal resignation as brigadier general and from his office of military governor. After Secretary of War Edwin Stanton received the resignation, he replied with a courteous message of praise for Johnson's performance. But Stanton, like Congressman Thaddeus Stevens, was soon to become Johnson's enemy and would be deeply involved in his downfall.

On the night of March 3, a party was held for Johnson by John Forney, the secretary of the Senate. Because Forney was a good friend, Johnson did not have the heart to turn down his invitation, even though he still felt feverish and dizzy. When Johnson awoke the next day, it was chilly and rainy. He was genuinely ill and also suffering from too much wine the night before. All in all, it was not a very promising start to such an important day.

Hannibal Hamlin, the departing Vice-President, rode down Pennsylvania Avenue in a carriage with Johnson, whose teeth chattered with fever and cold. When they arrived at the Capitol building and were safely inside the Vice-President's office, Johnson explained that his doctor had prescribed whiskey for his fever and asked Hamlin to get him some. Hamlin sent out for a bottle, and Johnson poured himself a tall drink. The inauguration ceremony lasted so long that he had time for another drink or two before it was his turn to make a speech to the Senate.

A Tipsy Vice-President

Members of the audience turned to one another with eyebrows raised in surprise when Johnson rose to make his first speech as Vice-President. His hair was ruffled, his face was red, his clothing seemed a bit disheveled, and he did not appear to be very steady on his feet. Then, when he began his speech, the looks of surprise turned to buzzing whispers of shocked astonishment. In a thick-tongued, slurred voice, the nation's new Vice-President launched into a rambling oration about his humble origins and the power of the common people.

Although Johnson meant to express his pride and his deep belief in American democracy, his speech lacked dignity and seemed merely an angry tirade. To make matters worse, he addressed individual senators, justices of the Supreme Court, diplomats, and other dignitaries by name, reminding them that, in the eyes of government, they were no better then the commoners. Many of them were deeply insulted by his personal remarks.

Johnson's tipsy appearance and belligerent manner caused a sensation in Washington. Senators were embarrassed; reporters, knowing a good story, were gleeful. Lincoln's reaction is not recorded, but he did whisper to one of the attendants that it would be best if Johnson did not appear with him on the outside porch of the Capitol after the oath-taking. So the new Vice-President was whisked away to a friend's house, where he spent two weeks recovering in seclusion while the capital and the nation buzzed with rumors of his drunkenness.

A Poor Beginning

Johnson was never able to live down the bad impression he made at the Capitol. Everyone, it seemed, had something to say about his intoxicated behavior at the inauguration. It was solemnly discussed by the Cabinet and the Congress, and it was mercilessly mocked by hostile newpapers. Johnson's friends and supporters declared, "The man was ill and exhausted. Why should one instance of poor judgment be held against a loyal servant of his country?"

Lincoln understood and forgave Johnson, saying, "I have known Andy for many years. He made a bad slip the other day, but you needn't be scared. He isn't a drunkard." Nevertheless, Johnson's enemies ever afterward accused him of alcoholism whenever he did something they did not like.

In truth, Johnson was not an alcoholic, although he did enjoy drinking and his sons' lives were troubled by drunkenness and alcoholism. It is also likely that his doctor had indeed recommended whiskey as medical treatment; the practice was common in those days. But his disturbing behavior on inauguration day was probably caused as much by fever, tiredness, and nervousness as by liquor.

The only person who said nothing about Johnson's behavior was Johnson himself. He was too proud, or too embarrassed, ever to refer to the matter. Gradually, however, the scandal died down, and Johnson was careful to drink nothing more than a single glass of wine on public occasions from then on.

VICE-PRESIDENT FOR FIVE WEEKS

The early weeks of President Lincoln's second term were busy but filled with promise. Although southern troops were putting up fierce resistance, the Confederacy was doomed. When word reached Washington that Union forces were on the verge of seizing the Confederate capital of Richmond, Virginia, Johnson cancelled a planned trip to Greeneville. It would have been his first visit home since he fled after Tennessee's secession, but he wanted to be in Washington for the war's end. Throughout the North, people's hearts lightened as they realized that the end was in sight.

About a month after the inauguration, Richmond fell to the North. Jefferson Davis, the Confederate president, fled from the city, along with other southern leaders, just before blue-coated Union soldiers swarmed into it. Johnson joined Lincoln in a somber visit to the former Confederate stronghold. They paced silently through the rooms of Davis' mansion and walked for a mile or so through the smoldering, shell-torn streets. But they did not swagger with the joy of triumphant conquerors. Instead, their expressions were sad as they gazed upon the ruins of a once-fine city, and their thoughts and words were concerned with the great task that lay ahead – the task of rebuilding the United States.

Lincoln's Hopes for Reconstruction

The decade that followed the Civil War has come to be known as the Age of Reconstruction. Lincoln had no illusions about Reconstruction; he knew that the task of bringing the North and the South together into a unified, harmonious nation would be at least as difficult as the task of winning the war.

So much had been changed by four years of war. States, communities, even families had been torn apart by conflicting loyalties. Hatreds had been born that would not die for generations. The North and South were cousins, if not brothers, and Lincoln remarked more than once that fights within families were more painful and harder to mend than fights between strangers. Hundreds of thousands had died, and the loss of homes, livestock, crops, and factories was enormous.

Slavery, the institution upon which the economic life of the South had rested for centuries, existed no longer. Perhaps the most fundamental change of all was that several million recently freed slaves had been given a new place in society, and no one was sure what to expect of them. In the meantime, they needed work, homes, and protection under the law.

Differences of Opinion

In view of all these upheavals, northern leaders were divided in their opinions as to how the South should be treated. There were almost as many thoughts about this as there were lawmakers, but the opinions generally fell into one of two opposing camps. In one camp were those who felt that the South should be punished and kept under military rule for some time, like any other conquered enemy. In the other camp were those who felt that to forgive and forget – to restore statehood and citizenship to the South as quickly as possible – was better than to punish.

The leader of those who wanted to reunite the country was President Lincoln. At his second inauguration, he said that it was time for northerners and southerners to move forward together "with malice toward none, with charity toward all . . . to bind up the nation's wounds." The North had beaten the South, but that did not give the North the right to withhold participation in government from the South.

From the start, Lincoln had favored a policy of mild Reconstruction, in which the only penalty for southerners would be the requirement of an oath of loyalty to the Union. At the time of his re-election, Lincoln had not yet worked out a detailed plan for Reconstruction as southern states and territories were reclaimed from the Confederacy. However, he did urge military governors of these states and territories to hasten the return to elected, civilian government and to show no unnecessary hostility toward the defeated southerners. Lincoln's basic views on the Reconstruction issue were quite clear to Johnson and to others.

Radical Views

The leader of the group that favored imposing harsh, punitive policies on the South was Representative Thaddeus Stevens of Pennsylvania, the leader of the Radical Republicans in Congress. Other congressional Radicals who agreed with Stevens were Charles Sumner and Ben Davis. In fact, all of the Radicals felt that the President's approach to Reconstruction was much too generous and soft-hearted.

In the century or so since Reconstruction, much has been said and written about the reasons for the Radicals' fierce stand against Lincoln's Reconstruction policy. One historian speculated that Stevens led the fight to punish the South because Confederate troops had passed through his hometown of Lancaster, Pennsylvania, and burned a factory that he owned. But whatever the personal motives of Stevens and the other Radicals, they are generally credited with two larger motives, one noble and the other not so admirable.

The virtuous goal was inherited from the old abolition movement. It was the desire to reform the entire social structure of the South. The Radicals feared, not without some reason, that although the black people of the South had been freed, they would still be held back by the whites, who would use low wages and discriminatory laws to keep blacks in a subordinate place. So, to some extent, the Radical approach to Reconstruction was aimed at protecting the newly freed blacks by stripping the whites of power.

But the Radicals also had another motive. They had never liked the Union Party, which was formed to win an election rather than because of shared ideals or beliefs. Stevens and the other Radical Republicans wanted to get power firmly back in the hands of the Republican Party—of themselves, in fact. Because Reconstruction was the most important political activity in the United States after the war, it was the main instrument of governmental power.

During Lincoln's first term, after Union troops took Louisiana, the Radicals had tried to pass a law that would have prevented the President from readmitting seceded states to the Union. Lincoln blocked this Radical move by vetoing the bill. He was able to wield enough political power to enforce his ideas about the early stages of Reconstruction—but just barely.

Johnson's Views

Johnson's position on Reconstruction at the time he took office as Vice-President was midway between the two extremes. He knew that the South had suffered terrible economic devastation in the war, and he did not feel that the southern people deserved the additional humiliation of having their statehood and citizenship withheld. At Lincoln's request, he had devoted two years of effort in Tennessee preparing that state to rejoin the Union and return to civilian government. He clearly felt that the South should be granted the same privileges of local government and representation in Congress that it had enjoyed before the war.

Yet Johnson remained as unsympathetic as ever to the wealthy southern class of plantation aristocrats, who had always been his enemies, and to those southern leaders who had deserted their posts in Congress when he risked so much to stay true to the Union. He blamed these Confederate aristocrats and leaders for the war, and he often said that they, not the common people of the South, were the ones who should be punished. He even spoke out in favor of hanging Jefferson Davis and other Confederate officers.

So, although he shared Lincoln's broad views about mild Reconstruction, Johnson also voiced some "fire and rope" opinions that pleased the Radicals. Despite his anger toward Davis, however, Johnson agreed far more closely with Lincoln than with the Radicals.

Not long after Richmond fell, Confederate General Robert E. Lee surrendered at Appomattox, Virginia, to Union General Ulysses S. Grant. The war was over, and Johnson looked forward to four years of helping Lincoln carry out his plans for Reconstruction. This dream was shattered with Lincoln's death on April 15. After all his struggles to end the war, Lincoln would not be the one to bind up the nation's wounds. But Johnson announced that he would carry out Lincoln's plans as he understood them.

JOHNSON TAKES CHARGE

In the days following Lincoln's assassination, Johnson had to cope with many critical governmental and political problems as well as with the changes in his personal life. As Vice-President, he had been content to room in Kirkwood House, while Eliza and the rest of his family remained in their homes in Greeneville. As President, however, he had to prepare to take up residence in the White House, so he sent for his family to join him.

A Large White House Family

Johnson did not move into the White House immediately. Mary Lincoln, the President's widow, was so paralyzed with grief that she could not organize her move out of the White House until early June. Johnson kindly told her to take as long as she needed. In the meantime, he stayed at the home of Representative Samuel Hooper of Massachusetts, with a temporary office in the Treasury Building.

Johnson finally moved into the White House on June 9, 1865. The big building seemed to echo the recent turmoil of war and the gloom of mourning. It was empty and rather lonely, for his family had not yet arrived in the nation's capital.

The first to arrive was his daughter Martha Patterson, with her husband and two children. A month later, in August, Eliza arrived. Still ill with tuberculosis, she retired to a quiet bedroom and left the official hostessing and the management of the household to Martha. The rest of the family consisted of Johnson's sons, Robert and Andrew; his widowed daughter, Mary Stover; and Mary's three children. Andrew, still a schoolboy, and five young grandchildren brought laughter and playfulness into the White House. They and their friends were a constant source of refreshment and good cheer for Johnson, who worked every day from about seven in the morning until midnight, with short breaks for a walk, dinner, and an evening snack with his family.

Martha Patterson—no stranger to the White House, as she had visited President Polk there during her girlhood—proved to be a capable and energetic substitute for the First Lady. She cleaned and redecorated the mansion's public and private rooms, which had grown dingy and shabby during the war years. And she started the tradition, which continues today, of using fresh flower arrangements from the White House greenhouses as decorations throughout the building.

Although Martha was a gracious and charming hostess on state occasions, she was not too proud to take a hand in domestic chores, from mending her own dresses to milking the two Jersey cows that the family kept on the White House grounds to provide fresh milk and butter. She made her father's home as informal, countryfied, and comfortable as possible, saying, "We are plain people from the mountains of Tennessee, called here for a short time by a national calamity. I trust too much will not be expected of us."

A Divided Cabinet

One of the first matters of state to which Johnson addressed himself was the Cabinet. Because he wanted to carry out Lincoln's plans for Reconstruction, Johnson decided to keep Lincoln's Cabinet, rather than appointing new members. In some ways, this was a mistake that would cost him dearly. Lincoln had been able to command the loyalty, or at least the obe-

Johnson (seated at the left) held his first Cabinet meeting in the Treasury Building on April 16, 1865. He wanted to keep Lincoln's Cabinet intact, but some Cabinet members later conspired in his downfall. (Library of Congress.)

dience, of his Cabinet members; Johnson could not. As the Johnson administration deteriorated into a battle between the President and the Congress, some of the Cabinet members allied themselves with the Radicals and worked against the President they were supposed to support.

Hugh McCulloch, secretary of the treasury, Edwin Stanton, secretary of war, James Speed, attorney general, and William Dennison, postmaster general, sided with the Radical Republicans. John Usher, secretary of the interior, resigned soon after Johnson became President; he was replaced by James Harlan, who then supported the Radicals. When Harlan resigned in 1866 to run for the Senate, he was replaced by Orville Browning, a Johnson supporter whose diaries are one of the best and most detailed records of political life in the Johnson administration. Johnson's other staunch allies in the Cabinet were William Seward, secretary of state, and Gideon Welles, secretary of the Navy.

A Sudden Turnabout

Surprisingly, in view of the antagonism that was to develop between Johnson and the Radicals, Johnson's first few months in office were marked by good relations with the Radicals and a high degree of popularity across the nation. The President made a number of speeches that were notable for their dignity, intelligence, and fairness; this pleased the people who had feared that they were governed by a drunken backwoods lout. He hastened the trial and punishment of the people who had conspired to kill President Lincoln and called for the hanging of Confederate leaders; this pleased the Radicals. Even Ben Wade, one of the most radical Republicans, said, "Johnson, by the gods we have faith in you."

Before long, however, the Republicans began to have doubts about Johnson. In May, he startled the Radicals by issuing proclamations that restored full rights and property to most southerners, officially recognized the new governments that Lincoln had set up in Tennessee, Arkansas, Louisiana, and Virginia, and paved the way for recognition of North Carolina and other states. When Democrats in the South praised his generous treatment of the southern states, Republicans remembered that he was, after all, a Democrat. Also damaging to Johnson's general reputation was the praise he received from Copperheads, or northerners who supported the Confederate cause during the war (hence, they were nicknamed for the poisonous snake).

At the end of 1865, Johnson's first year as President, much progress had been made toward the kind of mild, or

The Fate of the Conspirators

Like the assassination of President John F. Kennedy in 1963, Lincoln's assassination is wrapped in rumor and speculation. It is unlikely that the full story of the conspirators and their plot will ever be known.

Within hours of the shooting, federal agents, directed by Secretary of War Edwin Stanton, located a boardinghouse run by Mrs. Mary Surratt. John Wilkes Booth was known to have spent much time at the Surratt house meeting with John Surratt, Mrs. Surratt's son, who escaped to Italy before he could be arrested. Some of the roomers at the Surratt boardinghouse were believed to have been in on Booth's plan. Among them were Michael O'Laughlin and Samuel Arnold, former Confederate soldiers. They were arrested as they fled southward.

George Atzerodt, Johnson's would-be assassin, was captured, as was Lewis Payne, who had attacked Secretary of State William Seward. David Herold, who had helped Booth escape from Ford's Theatre, surrendered. Edward Spangler, an employee of the theater, and Samuel Mudd, a doctor who had set Booth's broken leg after the shooting, also were arrested. Two weeks after the assassination, Booth was tracked to a barn in Virginia. During a gun battle with federal agents, he either shot himself or was shot.

One of the most mysterious and interesting features of the events surrounding Lincoln's death is the role of Edwin Stanton. The secretary of war took charge of the investigation, persuaded Johnson to appoint a military court that would be under Stanton's control, rushed the trial, and did his best to use the assassination to stir up hatred against the South. He manipulated the evidence—including Booth's own diary—to suggest that Mary Surratt and some of the others knew that Booth had changed his plans from kidnapping to murder, when, in fact, it is likely that they did not know. And he created a web of evidence, some of it definitely false, that pointed toward Jefferson Davis and other high-ranking Confederates as the real authors of the plot. Ironically, it has been suggested by some later writers that Stanton himself was involved in the assassination, knowing that it would give him a powerful weapon against the South. But there is no more evidence against Stanton than against Davis.

Stanton's military court sentenced Atzerodt, Payne, and Herold to death by hanging. The same sentence was passed on Mrs. Surratt, but the court attached a recommendation for mercy. Stanton concealed this recommendation when he presented the sentences to Johnson to be signed, so she was hanged with the rest. Later, when Johnson discovered that Stanton had tricked him into having the woman hanged, the President was shocked and angry. This incident contributed to the hostility that developed between the two men.

For the rest of the conspirators, Spangler

received six years in prison and Arnold, O'Laughlin, and Dr. Mudd were sentenced to life in prison. Mudd's case is perhaps the saddest of them all. He stoutly maintained his innocence, claiming that he had simply treated an injured man without knowing who he was.

The doctor was sent to a federal prison in the Tortugas Islands, desolate little spits of sand near the Florida Keys. There he served valiantly as a prison doctor during an epidemic of the dreaded yellow fever, all the while proclaiming his innocence and pleading for a pardon. Yet he was so hated for helping Booth that his name became a synonym for a bad reputation. The phrase "His name is mud" started as "His name is Mudd." Today, historians are inclined to give Mudd the benefit of the doubt, and it is generally believed that he was innocent, as he claimed until his death.

lenient, Reconstruction that Lincoln had planned. Johnson appeared to be popular with the public and on good terms with Congress. But beneath the surface, hidden currents were directing the President and the Congress toward a long, bitter battle for power. The remainder of Johnson's administration would be dominated by that struggle, which would nearly cost him the Presidency.

Chapter 9

The President on Trial

Johnson's plan for Reconstruction was simple. He held the view that the southern states had never actually left the Union, because such an act is impossible under the Constitution. So he appointed a provisional governor for each state whose job was to oversee the administration of the oath of loyalty and, when enough citizens had taken the oath, to organize a state constitutional convention.

After each convention had drawn up a new state constitution – the only restriction being that the state had to ban slavery and secession – the state could elect its own government and representatives to Congress. Employing this procedure throughout 1865, Johnson accomplished much of the initial work of Reconstruction.

Johnson also wanted to allow each state to decide whether to give blacks the right to vote. (He favored giving the vote to educated blacks only, at least at first.) But southern whites, stinging from their defeat in the war, were not about to treat blacks as political equals. The southern states began enacting harsh laws, called Black Codes, that refused blacks the right to vote, to marry whites, or to work for the same wages as whites. This enraged northern Radical Republicans who complained that the condition of the blacks after the war was just as bad as slavery. To some extent, they were right. The Black Codes were cruel and unjust, especially in Mississippi and Louisiana. The Radical Republicans also feared that the South would become a stronghold of Democratic political power, and that the dominance achieved by the Republicans during the war would be eroded. For both of these reasons, the Radicals were determined not to work with Johnson to correct the very real problems of Reconstruction. Rather, they wanted to undo what he had done and take matters into their own hands.

SECRET MEETINGS AND OPEN WARFARE

Just before Congress met for a new session in December of 1865, Thaddeus Stevens and other Radicals held a secret meeting in Washington. They formed a plan that would keep the House of Representatives and the Senate from admitting the legislators who had been elected by the southern states. When Congress convened, both houses refused to seat the southerners, saying that the states had to be formally readmitted to the Union first. Then, at Stevens' suggestion, the two houses announced the formation of a Committee of Fifteen to prepare states for readmission, saying that the President had no authority to admit the states without congressional approval.

No one was fooled. This was more than a quibble over procedure. It was outright war between a small but powerful group in Congress and the President. Johnson did not help matters when, with his typical bluntness and impulsiveness, in an informal speech he openly accused Radicals Thad Stevens, Wendell Phillips, and Charles Sumner of trying to destroy the Union. This accusation removed any chance he might have had of settling his differences with the Radicals.

The Civil Rights Act

Within half a year, the Committee of Fifteen had blocked all of Johnson's attempts to continue Reconstruction according to his plan. Congress then passed a Civil Rights Act that gave blacks the right to vote but took away the vote from many whites on the grounds that they had rebelled against the government. The Radicals not only wanted to prevent many white Democrats from voting, but also to create many new black voters, who would then be certain to vote for Republican candidates out of gratitude.

Johnson was not absolutely opposed to giving blacks the right to vote, but he did not want that same right withheld from whites. In addition, he still felt that the states should be allowed to make the decision for themselves. For these reasons, he vetoed the act. Congress, however, passed the act over his veto and incorporated it into the Constitution as the 14th Amendment.

Congress also passed a law saying that no southern state could be readmitted to the Union until it had accepted the 14th Amendment. This meant that the southern states had no rights to self-government or to representation in the federal government until they had agreed to the Republicans' terms. Only Tennessee accepted the amendment at once. The governor, Parson Brownlow, once again turned against Johnson and sided with the Radical Republicans, many of whom were his old allies from the Whig Party.

"A Swing 'Round the Circle"

Although it was not a presidential election year, 1866 was an important campaign year. Because elections of senators and representatives would determine the makeup of Congress for the next two years, Johnson hoped that the Union Party had enough life left in it to get some of its candidates elected. At a Union Party convention held in Philadelphia in August, the delegates announced their support of President Johnson and mild Reconstruction, but it was clear that the party had no real political strength left. Important people had deserted it for the Democratic or Republican parties, and some districts did not even send delegates to the convention. Outsiders criticized the convention as a nest of Copperheads, and to some extent they were right.

Johnson decided that other measures were needed to win popular support for his policies. Throughout his career, he had achieved his greatest triumphs as a stump speaker, taking his case to the people and addressing them in his vigorous, direct manner. The strategy that had served him so well in Tennessee politics, he felt, could now be turned to national use. He decided to make what was called "a swing 'round the circle," or a railroad tour of the major cities, making speeches at every stop.

Although Johnson had high hopes for his speaking tour, it was a disaster. Perhaps the rough-and-ready oratory that had worked in Tennessee no longer appealed to a nation made weary and disillusioned by war. Or perhaps Johnson, older now and very tired, had lost some of his crowd-pleasing skill.

It is known that the Radicals planted hecklers in the crowds in many cities where Johnson spoke. Their jeers so provoked the President in Cincinnati that he broke into angry abuse of the audience. Riots and fistfights followed nearly every one of his speeches, which grew louder and angrier as the tour progressed.

Newspaper reporters took advantage of the opportunity to show Johnson as crude and arrogant, instructing voters across the land to do as he told them. Like his hero, Andrew Jackson, he was called "King Andy" in the press; cartoons showed him wearing a crown and a tipsy leer. The old accusations of his drunkenness surfaced again, and the tour was portrayed as an unruly, liquor-fueled procession.

The Polar Bear Garden

Johnson's presidency was dominated by his struggles with Congress and his impeachment, just as Lincoln's was dominated by the Civil War. Because we usually think of Johnson as "the President who was impeached," we sometimes forget the significant achievements of his administration. Nebraska achieved statehood in 1867. That same year, Secretary of State William Seward announced the United States claim to the Midway Islands, a small group of islands in the Pacific Ocean that would be of great strategic value in World War II. But by far, the crowning accomplishment of both Johnson and Seward was the purchase of Alaska.

Perched high on the edge of the North American continent, a few miles from Russia across the Bering Strait and northwest of British Canada, the province of Alaska had been colonized by Russian fur traders during the 1700s. Although both England and Spain had sent ships into Alaskan waters and had tried to establish outposts in Alaska, Russian control remained firm.

In the 1850s, however, Russia was at war with England and needed money. In addition, the Russian capital at St. Petersburg was in European Russia, far from Alaska. When the Russian ruler, Tsar Alexander II, grew tired of the cost of maintaining and defending a colony on the other side of the world, he decided to sell it. Although the British were eager to add Alaska to Canada, Alexander did not intend for them to get it. He offered it to the Americans in 1857, but the Civil War interrupted negotiations.

Early in 1867, the Russian ambassador to Washington brought the matter up again. Seward was in favor of the idea, claiming that Alaska would be an invaluable source of land and natural resources. Also, he did not want the British to get it, either. So, without waiting for Congress' approval, Seward hastily arranged a treaty of sale, which President Johnson promptly signed. It gave the United States 586,400 square miles—an area equal to one-fifth of the area of the 48 mainland states—for $7,200,000, or about two cents an acre, a deal that ranks with the Louisiana Purchase as an outstanding example of shrewd real-estate shopping. Although Congress dallied for more than a year, it finally approved the expenditure.

In the meantime, however, control of Alaska passed to the United States in October of 1867. Sitka, the Russian trading capital, became the center of the American administration, and the Russian residents were given three years to return to Russia. Most left, but those who remained became American citizens.

As the subject of countless television documentaries and magazine articles, Alaska is pretty well known to most Americans today. But in 1867 it was a land of utter mystery. People pictured it as a perpetual wilderness of ice and snow, populated by savages, polar bears, and walruses. No one would have believed that it would one day be regarded as a national treasure for its magnificent scenery and abundance of resources.

Newspapers of the time dubbed the purchase "Seward's Folly" ("folly" means "foolishness") and called Alaska "Andy's Polar Bear Garden" and "Walrussia." Congress — led by Thad Stevens, of course — raged that Johnson had once again exceeded his authority (President Thomas Jefferson had faced the same accusation regarding the Louisiana Purchase in 1803). But the American people did not seem to resent the purchase of Alaska, and many of them felt that anything was better than letting England acquire it.

Alaska was administered by the War Department and the Treasury Department until 1884, when it became a land district with a governor and a district court. It was designated as a territory of the United States in 1912 and achieved statehood in 1958. The United States owes its largest state, and one of its most beautiful and promising, to William Seward's foresight and Andrew Johnson's willingness to take decisive action, with or without the help of Congress.

One aspect of the tour that became important later was that General Grant, who had accompanied Johnson, was well received by the crowds and began to have political ambitions of his own. But a more immediate result was Johnson's failure to make any friends for himself or his program of Reconstruction. In fact, the ill-judged swing 'round the circle may have cost him some support, for the election of 1866 sent many Radicals to Congress.

BLACK RECONSTRUCTION

In 1867 the Radical-dominated Congress proceeded to undo all Reconstruction work that had been started by Lincoln and continued by Johnson. The new state governments were disbanded, and the new state constitutions were discarded. The South was divided into five military districts, each commanded by a general appointed by Congress. Congress also set the guidelines for voter registration and for the drafting of another set of constitutions. Federal soldiers occupied the South.

Whites in the South were outraged, claiming that they were being taxed and oppressed by a government that denied them representation, but few northerners cared about their point of view. Ironically, Lincoln's death had turned the country against his own lenient approach to Reconstruction. In the eyes of the North, southerners had killed the President, so they were in no position to make demands.

Many northerners, in fact, came to believe that southerners had no rights. This treatment seemed particularly harsh to southern whites because it followed a year or so of lenient, peaceful treatment and because it violated all the promises made to the South by Lincoln and Johnson. Because of the hatred that it spawned among both northerners and southerners, the troubled decade that followed 1867 is sometimes called Black Reconstruction.

Carpetbaggers, Scalawags, and the Klan

One feature of Black Reconstruction that was particularly despised in the South was the horde of northern administrators and petty officials who flowed south to take jobs in the

Reconstruction bureaucracy. Although some of them were honest, capable people, many were ignorant, lazy scoundrels whose purpose was to line their pockets with bribes and fat salaries while doing as little constructive work as possible. These greedy, self-serving rascals were called Carpetbaggers, after the cheap bags made of old pieces of carpet in which they carried their clothes as they piled aboard southbound trains.

But the Carpetbaggers had their counterparts in the South. As in any conquered territory, there were plenty of people willing to collaborate with the conquerors in scheming for money or advancement. Many southerners joined the Carpetbaggers in plundering the South; these people were called Scalawags (an old-fashioned word that means "knave" or "rascal").

The Carpetbaggers and Scalawags did much damage to the South's pride and its economy, but at least they disappeared after a decade or two. Another feature of post-Civil War life in the South is still with us today. It is the Ku Klux Klan, an organization founded in Pulaski, Tennessee, in 1866 by a group of white men who enjoyed dressing up as ghosts to frighten the free blacks of the area. A year later, however, a much larger and more sinister version of the Klan was organized in Nashville. It called itself "the invisible empire of the South" and was dedicated to preserving white power and hampering the government of the free blacks and Carpetbaggers. It did so through threats, beatings, rigged juries, and murder.

It is sometimes forgotten that other secret societies, such as the Union League and the Loyal League, were formed in the South by Carpetbaggers to control the black vote, and that these groups also used underhanded and violent methods. The Klan opposed these societies, as did other white-supremacy groups that flourished in the South during Reconstruction.

The Klan, however, is the only such group known to still be active today. Its symbol is a burning cross, which has often been used to terrorize blacks and those whites who sympathize with them. Fortunately, both the membership and the power of the Klan have declined sharply since the civil rights movement of the 1960s.

IMPEACHMENT

With dwindling support in Congress and among the people, Johnson strove to halt Congress in its stern, vengeful course. He stood true to Lincoln's original plan for Reconstruction, partly because he thought it was fair and partly out of sympathy for the suffering of the South. Principally, however, he felt that, in taking control over Reconstruction, Congress was tampering with the very nature of constitutional democracy in America.

The Constitution established a system of checks and balances to distribute power equally between the executive branch of government (the President), the legislative branch (Congress), and the judicial branch (the Supreme Court). Now Congress had tipped that essential balance. Furthermore, Congress was governing citizens without their consent and without allowing them to be represented in that lawmaking body. This, to Johnson, was baldly unconstitutional. Even Thad Stevens, who stated plainly that his goal was to put the Republican Party on top for a long time to come, admitted that Congress had set the Constitution aside for a while—out of necessity, he said.

Johnson, however, did not believe that any necessity could justify overriding the document that gave life to the United States government. And he did not believe that party power or party loyalty should be more important than the good of all the people. Therefore, he tried in every way possible to make life difficult for the Radicals, vetoing 29 of their bills (15 of them were passed over his veto) and generally obstructing their plans. So they decided to get rid of him.

As early as December of 1866, some Radicals had begun to talk about impeaching Johnson — that is, charging him with official misconduct. If he were found guilty of such charges, he could be removed from office. No President of the United States had ever been impeached; indeed, impeachment had always been regarded as an extremely serious matter. But the Radicals were almost comical in their attempts to impeach Johnson.

The first attempt was by Representative James Ashley of Ohio, who accused Johnson of being part of the plot to assassinate Lincoln. This charge was so ridiculous and offensive that the Speaker of the House, who hated Johnson, had to criticize Ashley. Other wild accusations followed, but the Radicals simply could not produce any worthy evidence of wrongdoing on Johnson's part. Then, in an incident both laughable and pitiful, Johnson played into their hands and gave them the ammunition they needed to bring him to trial.

The War at the War Department

One of the laws that Congress passed over Johnson's veto in 1867 was called the Tenure of Office Act. It said that the President could not dismiss public officials, including Cabinet members whom he had appointed, without the consent of Congress. The privilege of appointing and dismissing Cabinet members had always fallen to the President, and Johnson saw no reason why that should change. But Congress had passed the act in order to protect those Cabinet members who were secretly working against the President. The chief of these was Secretary of War Edwin Stanton.

In the summer of 1867, Johnson learned of Stanton's dishonesty in hiding the mercy recommendation for Mary Surratt. He demanded Stanton's resignation and appointed General Grant as his successor. This was a double mistake. Not only did Johnson's dismissal of Stanton allow the Radicals to accuse him of violating the Tenure of Office Act, but, unknown to Johnson, Grant himself was sympathetic to the Radicals and no longer wanted to be identified with Johnson's administration. So Grant was little help to Johnson. When Grant discovered that his appointment as secretary of war would pit him against the Radicals, he resigned in a curt note to Johnson.

The next step was a melodrama at the War Department. Hearing of Grant's resignation, Stanton rushed to his old office, seized the key, and barricaded himself inside. He lived there for weeks, with the doors locked and guards placed around the building to prevent Johnson from having him removed by force. The Radicals sent Stanton meals of his favorite dishes as they cheerfully planned Johnson's impeachment.

On February 24, 1868, the House of Representatives voted 126 to 47 in favor of impeaching President Andrew Johnson. He was to stand trial before the Senate on 11 charges of misconduct. The most important charges concerned his alleged violation of the Tenure of Office Act. The other charges were trivial — including one that he had made the office of the President appear undignified by speaking in a loud voice! If found guilty, Johnson could be removed from office, fined $10,000, and even imprisoned for five years.

The President asked for 40 days to prepare his defense but was given 10. With the help of Henry Stanbery, who had replaced James Speed as attorney general in 1866, and Wil-

Radical Thaddeus Stevens, who despised Johnson, delivered a passionate speech at the end of the impeachment debate in the House of Representatives. The House then voted 126 to 47 to put the President on trial. (Library of Congress.)

liam Evarts, who became attorney general upon Stanbery's resignation, Johnson set about the hasty preparations for his day in court.

The Trial

Throughout the trial the Senate galleries were packed with spectators. So many people fought for seats that the Senate had to issue tickets, most of which were sold at high prices to foreign diplomats, society women, politicians, or anyone else who could afford them. After all, Johnson's trial was possibly the most exciting thing that had ever happened in American politics.

Radical representatives made passionate speeches in favor of conviction. Johnson's lawyers made equally passionate speeches in favor of acquittal. Johnson's voice, however, was not heard. His lawyers and loyal Cabinet members had advised him not to appear, because they felt that his presence would give the occasion more dignity than it deserved and would simply entertain the curious crowds.

So Johnson, who was always a man who wanted to confront his accusers face to face and tell them what he thought of them, reluctantly agreed to wait out the tense two weeks of the trial in his office. At the end of each day, someone from the defense team ran from the Capitol to the White House to report the day's happenings to Johnson.

On the last day of the hearing, Representative J. A. Bingham summed up the case for convicting Johnson. He was so eloquent that he brought the crowd in the Senate galleries to its feet, cheering and yelling. Chief Justice Salmon P. Chase, who was presiding over the impeachment hearing, pounded his gavel and demanded order. Although he was no admirer of Johnson, Justice Chase insisted that the hearing be carried out in a fair and orderly manner. But the crowd became so unruly that the Senate guards had to shove people outdoors to restore order. After that outburst, the Senate adjourned for several months. The senators would vote on the charges when the Senate reconvened in May.

The Vote

At that time, the Senate had 54 members. For Johnson to be convicted, 36 of them would have to find him guilty. Because the Radicals had never controlled the Senate as effectively as the House of Representatives, they were not certain that they could get 36 votes for conviction. But they had one more trick up their sleeves. When the Senate met to vote on the impeachment charges, the Radicals arranged for the vote to begin with the 11th charge, which was the last and most serious one. They were afraid that if the more trivial charges were read first, many senators would vote "Not guilty," and that might influence the vote on the most important charge.

The galleries were packed on May 16, but a hush fell over the Senate as the charge was read and the voting began. Each senator's name was called, and each called out his vote in reply. Tension mounted as first William Fessenden of Maine and then James Grimes of Iowa, both Republicans, defied their party's orders and cried out, "Not guilty!" The Radicals held their breaths in dismay—maybe Johnson had a chance of surviving.

In all, seven brave Republicans crossed party lines to join the Democratic senators in voting "Not guilty." The end result was 35 votes for conviction, 19 for acquittal. The Radicals had failed by one vote.

Colonel William Crook, Johnson's bodyguard, sped to the White House and burst into the President's office, shouting, "Mr. President, you are acquitted!" Johnson broke down and wept. Then, for the first time in many months, he raised a glass of whiskey in a victory toast.

Chapter **10**

Return to Tennessee

Although he was acquitted of all charges, Johnson's impeachment ended his political career. In truth, while he would like to have been nominated to run again, he did not expect it. Because too much controversy surrounded his presidency, the Democrats wanted to start anew with someone else. When they met for their national convention six weeks after the impeachment trial ended, the Democrats nominated Horatio Seymour of New York as their candidate for President. The Union Party was dead. The Republicans nominated Grant, Lincoln's general and Johnson's one-time supporter who had allied himself with the Radicals.

Grant won a hearty majority at the polls in November. The Republican victory was based on "waving the bloody shirt of the rebellion," or blaming the southern Democrats for the war, and on the manipulation of black voters by the Carpetbaggers. Still, it brought Grant to the White House.

By now, relations between Johnson and Grant were poor. Nevertheless, Johnson invited Grant to his final formal event as President, a White House reception on New Year's Eve. Grant did not come, so Johnson did not attend his successor's inauguration in March. Instead, he spent his final hours in the White House drawing up meticulous notes about items that needed Grant's attention. Eliza and the rest of Johnson's family had already left for Tennessee. At noon, just as Grant was taking his oath of office, Johnson left the White House for the last time.

RETURN TO GREENEVILLE

Andrew Johnson was not a man to hide his honest opinions for appearance's sake. In his last message to Congress, in December of 1868, he refused to settle for a few meaningless parting words. He called Congress' Reconstruction scheme "a failure" and a betrayal of Lincoln's plans for the nation. Many Radical leaders walked out on the speech, and there were even attempts to keep it from being printed and distributed, as was the custom. Johnson left office speaking his mind and stirring up trouble, just as he always had.

Even so, he must have been deeply pleased to find that his home town of Greeneville welcomed him with respect and affection. Across the main street, where eight years earlier a banner had branded him a traitor, hung a banner that read "Andrew Johnson, Patriot." With Eliza and his surviving children and grandchildren, the 61-year-old President settled down in the home he had not seen for many years.

New Campaigns

But Johnson did not plan to retire quietly into sleepy old age. He was bitterly resentful of the slurs against his name and his policies that he had endured in his career. He wanted to disprove the charges against him once and for all by regaining public confidence—and a public office. He became involved in the activities of the Democratic Party in Tennessee and ran for the U.S. Senate in 1869 and then the House of Representatives in 1871; he was defeated both times.

Johnson died in 1875, a few months after his re-election to the U.S. Senate. He was buried wrapped in an American flag, with his head resting upon a copy of the Constitution. (Library of Congress.)

In 1872, he dusted off his old bag of stump-speaking tricks and campaigned on behalf of newspaper editor Horace Greeley for President; Greeley was defeated. Nonetheless, Johnson was called into service again in 1874, to make speeches for various Democratic candidates for congressional seats.

A Final Victory

Despite his two defeats, Johnson's own political ambitions were not yet dead. In 1874 he declared himself a candidate for the Senate seat held by Parson Brownlow. In January of 1875, after 55 hotly contested ballots, the state legislature of Tennessee cast a majority vote for Johnson.

The former President, the first ever to become a Senator after his presidency, arrived in Washington in March. He made only one speech on the floor of the Senate; it was an attack on Grant's handling of Reconstruction and on the corruption that pervaded the former general's administration. "Let us lay aside our party feelings," he urged his fellow senators. "Let us lay aside our personalities and come up to the Constitution of our country and lay it upon an altar and all stand around, resolved that the Constitution shall be preserved."

Those were Johnson's last public words. Congress adjourned the next day, and he went home to Tennessee. Sometime in June he wrote a note to himself that suggests that he had achieved peace of mind at last. "I have performed my duty to God, my country, and my family," it said. "I have nothing to fear in approaching death." A few weeks later, while visiting his daughter Mary and his grandchildren, he suffered two strokes in two days. He died on July 31, 1875.

Johnson was buried on August 3 on a hilltop in Greeneville. His body was wrapped in an American flag, and his head rested upon a copy of the Constitution. A simple stone monument was placed above his grave bearing the words "His faith in the people never wavered."

A NEW VIEW

For many years, Johnson was remembered — if at all — as the only President who has ever been impeached (impeachment proceedings were begun against President Richard Nixon, but he resigned before the trial started). The image of Johnson that lingered in people's minds was one that had been promoted by his enemies — that of a tough-talking, hard-drinking, stubborn President who fought Congress at every turn. There are some elements of truth in that image. Today, however, the opinion of most scholars and historians is that Johnson, although not a great President, was a better President than previously judged.

Many scholars and historians feel that the well-being of both North and South, of both black and white, would have been much greater during the past century if Johnson's plans for Reconstruction had been followed. And some claim that it was only his sturdy resistance that prevented the power-crazed Radical Congress from doing further damage to the country, perhaps even altering its constitutional form of democracy permanently.

True, Johnson was loud, easily angered, stubborn, and tactless. He lacked the powers of compromise, negotiation, and diplomacy that may be especially important to leaders in troubled times. But he was also honest, loyal, and fiercely dedicated to democracy. By modern standards, he would be considered a racist, although nowhere near as bad a one as many people in the 19th century were. By the standards of his own time, however, he was relatively moderate in his views about race, neither an abolitionist nor a white supremacist like the Klansmen. And by anybody's standards, his life story was a miracle of energy, ambition, and determination that carried him from a pauper's shack to the White House.

In short, Andrew Johnson was no saint, nor was he a villain, as his enemies claimed. Like most people, he was somewhere in the middle. But, unlike most people, he was tested by dire poverty, war, personal attacks, betrayals, and public humiliation on a grand scale. In the face of all this, he did his best to be true to what he believed.

Bibliography

Goodman, Walter. *Black Bondage: The Life of Slaves in the South.* New York: Farrar, Straus & Giroux, 1969. Illustrated with old photographs, paintings, and etchings, this 148-page book gives an introduction to slavery in the South before the Civil War.

Hoyt, Edwin P. *Andrew Johnson.* Chicago: Reilly & Lee, 1965. A concise and readable summary of Johnson's life and deeds. Hoyt presents Johnson as a heroic figure who defended the Constitution and the presidency against the misguided and unscrupulous Radical Republicans. The picture is a little one-sided, but there is much truth in it.

Lomask, Milton. *Andrew Johnson: President on Trial.* New York: Farrar, Straus, 1960. Although it covers Johnson's whole life, this book is really about the events, plots, and conflicts leading up to the President's impeachment. It gives a detailed day-by-day account of the impeachment proceedings.

Severn, Bill. *In Lincoln's Footsteps: The Life of Andrew Johnson.* New York: Ives Washburn, 1966. This book is aimed at young adult readers. It has a brisk, lively style, especially in the chapters dealing with Johnson's early life and career. The emphasis is on Johnson's place in the broad political picture of the times. Lincoln and other individuals who played important roles in Johnson's life are profiled briefly.

Trelease, Allen. *Reconstruction: The Great Experiment.* New York: Harper & Row, 1971. For readers unfamiliar with the eventful chapter of United States history that immediately followed the Civil War, this book is a comprehensive overview of the personalities and problems of Reconstruction. Johnson's battles with the Radical Republicans is one of the main themes.

Index

PRESIDENTS OF THE UNITED STATES

GEORGE WASHINGTON	L. Falkof	0-944483-19-4
JOHN ADAMS	R. Stefoff	0-944483-10-0
THOMAS JEFFERSON	R. Stefoff	0-944483-07-0
JAMES MADISON	B. Polikoff	0-944483-22-4
JAMES MONROE	R. Stefoff	0-944483-11-9
JOHN QUINCY ADAMS	M. Greenblatt	0-944483-21-6
ANDREW JACKSON	R. Stefoff	0-944483-08-9
MARTIN VAN BUREN	R. Ellis	0-944483-12-7
WILLIAM HENRY HARRISON	R. Stefoff	0-944483-54-2
JOHN TYLER	L. Falkof	0-944483-60-7
JAMES K. POLK	M. Greenblatt	0-944483-04-6
ZACHARY TAYLOR	D. Collins	0-944483-17-8
MILLARD FILLMORE	K. Law	0-944483-61-5
FRANKLIN PIERCE	F. Brown	0-944483-25-9
JAMES BUCHANAN	D. Collins	0-944483-62-3
ABRAHAM LINCOLN	R. Stefoff	0-944483-14-3
ANDREW JOHNSON	R. Stevens	0-944483-16-X
ULYSSES S. GRANT	L. Falkof	0-944483-02-X
RUTHERFORD B. HAYES	N. Robbins	0-944483-23-2
JAMES A. GARFIELD	F. Brown	0-944483-63-1
CHESTER A. ARTHUR	R. Stevens	0-944483-05-4
GROVER CLEVELAND	D. Collins	0-944483-01-1
BENJAMIN HARRISON	R. Stevens	0-944483-15-1
WILLIAM McKINLEY	D. Collins	0-944483-55-0
THEODORE ROOSEVELT	R. Stefoff	0-944483-09-7
WILLIAM H. TAFT	L. Falkof	0-944483-56-9
WOODROW WILSON	D. Collins	0-944483-18-6
WARREN G. HARDING	A. Canadeo	0-944483-64-X
CALVIN COOLIDGE	R. Stevens	0-944483-57-7

HERBERT C. HOOVER	B. Polikoff	0-944483-58-5
FRANKLIN D. ROOSEVELT	M. Greenblatt	0-944483-06-2
HARRY S. TRUMAN	D. Collins	0-944483-00-3
DWIGHT D. EISENHOWER	R. Ellis	0-944483-13-5
JOHN F. KENNEDY	L. Falkof	0-944483-03-8
LYNDON B. JOHNSON	L. Falkof	0-944483-20-8
RICHARD M. NIXON	R. Stefoff	0-944483-59-3
GERALD R. FORD	D. Collins	0-944483-65-8
JAMES E. CARTER	D. Richman	0-944483-24-0
RONALD W. REAGAN	N. Robbins	0-944483-66-6
GEORGE H.W. BUSH	R. Stefoff	0-944483-67-4

GARRETT EDUCATIONAL CORPORATION
130 EAST 13TH STREET
ADA, OK 74820

DATE DUE
